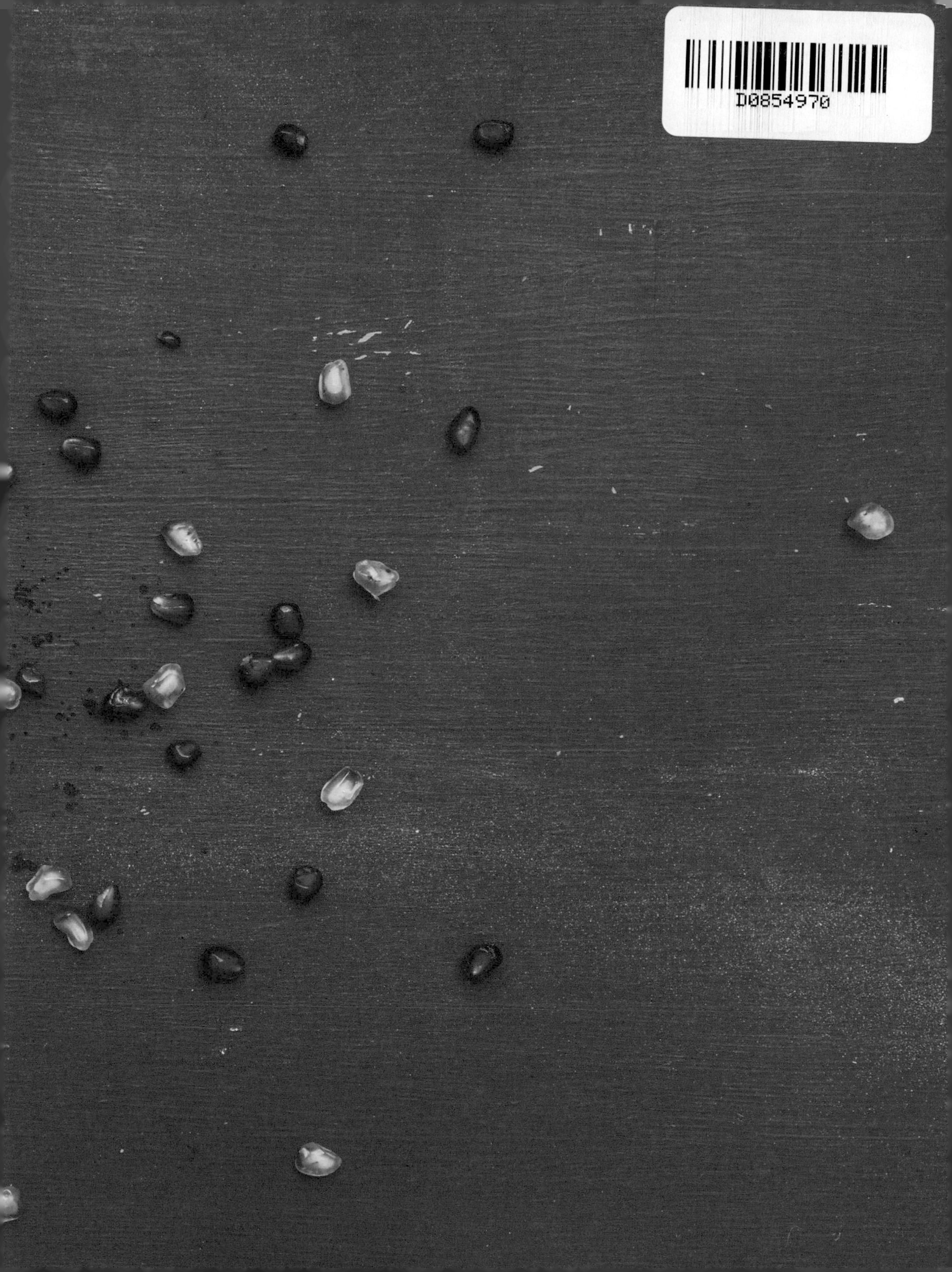

Persiana

Recipes from the Middle East & beyond

For my mother—loving, supportive, and always
ready to try whatever concoction I place in front of
her. Love you Mama… even if you still can't cook.

Persiana

Recipes from the Middle East & beyond

Sabrina Ghayour

Interlink Books

An imprint of Interlink Publishing Group, Inc.
Northampton, Massachusetts

Contents

8 ✻ Mezze & sharing plates
50 ✻ Breads & grains
74 ✻ Soups, stews & tagines
100 ✻ Roasts & grills
148 ✻ Salads & vegetables
206 ✻ Desserts & sweet treats
234 ✻ Index
240 ✻ Acknowledgments

Introduction

Middle Eastern cooking is often shrouded in mystery—it's the stuff of Arabian nights and full of Eastern promise. It is perceived as exotic and unknown. But this is not a true reflection of the simple and honest cuisine that it is. Perhaps the misconception is due to something being lost in translation… if a dish has a Persian, Turkish, or Arabic name, you might think "Well, that must be really hard to make…" when, in essence, there is little complexity involved in many of the recipes.

I began cooking at the tender age of six and, while I would love to say that I learned everything I know from my mother or grandmother, I can tell you that I am, in fact, a self-taught cook. Nobody in my household really knew how to cook, so home cooking consisted of a handful of dishes often thrown together out of convenience or necessity rather than joy or love of feeding people. Experimenting in the kitchen was commonplace for me and, by my late teens, I decided it was time to teach myself how to cook Persian food, which is exactly what I did. At first, my focus was strictly Persian, but growing up in a family that enjoyed influences from the Turkish, Arab, Armenian, and Afghani cultures and cuisines meant that my repertoire naturally grew over time.

Fast forward to the present and I have found every shortcut possible to simplify many Persian and Middle Eastern recipes, to create a style of cooking that fits comfortably into my everyday life. Although some recipes in this book are authentic, some draw inspiration from the Middle East and combine the wonderful flavors and ingredients of the region with everyday produce that's available in supermarkets everywhere. You don't need to have a million ingredients to create something delicious and special—sometimes you just need a handful of spices, and a few helpful hints on what to do with them and how versatile they can be. This alone can transform how you cook at home.

I host supper clubs at various venues in London and it never fails to surprise me just how successfully a table of food can bring people together. Guests arrive as complete strangers and leave the table as friends—and this is exactly what food is for us. It provides a convivial experience, during which all else is put aside and food and enjoyment become the focus. In the Middle East, food is not just about sustenance. There is a sense of occasion, a sense of unity that goes with it. You create a feast for your guests to show them you value them, to make them feel special. You form bonds and build lasting relationships over food, much the way that so many other cultures like to celebrate with wine and drinks.

I can understand that the way we eat in the Middle East can be overwhelming for some cultures. We do like to fill the table with a myriad of dishes both hot and cold, with an abundance of color, variety, and both meat and vegetables. Of course, not every day has to be a banquet. Some days I just want a simple one-pot recipe that will feed the family quickly and easily, and on other days, I feel like preparing a feast. Whichever way you like to eat, in this book there is something to suit your every mood and plenty of variety to suit every palate.

Growing up in an Iranian family, Persian food will always be my first love, but I was raised in England and, having lived here for over 30 years, I consider myself to be British. My style of cooking is very much based on ingredients that can easily be found in supermarkets, along with a few ingredients here and there that may require a bit more of a search (unless you have a Middle Eastern grocery store nearby) or you can always order them online. It's important you don't feel as if every recipe must be replicated with 100 percent accuracy—in all honesty, the best recipes are those that are born through an accidental occurrence, such as substituting an ingredient for one that was required. This is the way in which to build confidence and demystify Middle Eastern cooking. If you like cumin, add cumin! If you don't like it, then leave it out. You won't ruin a recipe by replacing or omitting an ingredient here and there.

Flavorful food needn't be a chore, and if you know what to do with a few simple store-cupboard ingredients, you can do wonders in the kitchen. If you were to cook a recipe that was too ingredient- or labor-intensive, what would be the chances of you making that recipe again? Slim—be honest. I have found that if you keep a few spices in your pantry, some preserved lemons and maybe some harissa, magical, wonderful things can happen... Even on those nights when you are stuck in traffic, come home an hour later than planned, but STILL want to eat something delicious for dinner, you can put something special on the table without breaking a sweat.

No mess, no fuss, just simple and delicious food—that's what I like to eat, that's what I like to cook for my family and friends, and that's just what I want to share with you. I hope this book shows you that the food, flavors, and ingredients of the Middle East are accessible and uncomplicated, and therefore far more achievable than you might have previously believed.

Sabrina Ghayour

Mezze & sharing plates

Fava beans with Garlic, Dill & Eggs
Baghala Ghatogh

This dish hails from the northern provinces of Iran. The first time I had this dish as a youngster, it blew my mind. I had never tried anything quite like it; fiercely garlicky and ridiculously tasty, it is not a very mainstream Persian dish, which explains why it was so alien to me at the time. Now when I make it, I sometimes stir the mixture into cooked white rice and I find this the most satisfying rice dish you could ever want to eat.

SERVES 4 AS PART OF A MEZZE

olive oil

1 garlic bulb, cloves bashed and thinly sliced

2¼lb (1kg) shelled fresh or frozen fava beans, skins removed

3 tsp turmeric

generous 1 tsp crushed sea salt flakes (less if using table salt)

freshly ground black pepper

1 large bunch or 3 x ¾oz/20g packets of dill, stalks and leaves finely chopped

pat of butter (about 2 tbsp/25g)

4 large free-range eggs

∂ Heat a large deep frying pan over low-medium heat, add a generous drizzle of olive oil, and sweat the garlic until it softens and becomes slightly translucent. Add the fava beans and increase the heat to medium, then add the turmeric, sea salt, and some black pepper and stir well. After 5 minutes, mix in the chopped dill and cook for a further 8 minutes or so.

∂ Add the butter to the pan and let it melt into the beans. Crack the eggs onto the surface of the beans in different areas and allow them to cook through using the heat from the beans. Give the pan a shake to distribute the egg whites. This will take about 15 minutes, at which point the beans will have changed from a bright green to a slightly more dull green—but don't panic because this is how they should be. Serve this dish with Persian Flatbread (*see* page 55), which is perfect for scooping up the delicious garlicky beans and soft oozy eggs. Alternatively, serve with naan or flour tortilla wraps.

Eggplant *Chermoula*

Originally a North African spice paste, *chermoula* can be used as a rub, seasoning, or base to flavor many a dish. I use some of the key spices to make this dish and the end result is best described as tangy, sweet, fresh, and chutney-like. It is quite similar to the Sicilian *caponata*, which I adore, but the spices in my Eggplant *Chermoula* give it added depth. For me, its distinct sweet and sour character makes this dish impossible to resist and highly addictive.

SERVES 6 AS PART OF A MEZZE

olive oil

2 eggplants, trimmed and cut into 1in (2.5cm) cubes

sea salt

½ large onion, cut in half and thinly sliced into half moons

3 garlic cloves, crushed into a paste with some salt

1 tsp ground cumin

½ tsp ground cinnamon

1 tsp sweet paprika

½ red pepper, cored, deseeded, and cut lengthways into thin strips, then halved

handful of plump golden raisins

1 x 14oz/400g chopped tomatoes

3 tbsp red wine vinegar

2 tsp superfine sugar

2 tbsp runny honey

∂ Heat a good glug of olive oil in a saucepan over medium heat, then add the eggplant and sauté until golden brown. Season with salt halfway through. Once browned but not blackened, remove the eggplant from the pan and set aside.

∂ Put the pan back on the heat, reduce the temperature to low, add the onion slices, and cook until caramelized, ensuring you stir them so that they cook and color evenly. Just as they start to brown, add the garlic paste, cumin, cinnamon, and paprika and stir, then add the pepper strips and continue to sauté until the vegetables soften and the peppers are no longer raw. Add the raisins and a touch more salt and fry for a further 5 minutes before adding the chopped tomatoes. Cook for another 5 minutes, then add the red wine vinegar, sugar, and honey.

∂ Increase the temperature and stir-fry the mixture for a minute or two (ensuring it doesn't burn), then reduce the temperature to low and, using a potato masher, lightly mash the mixture and stir it to ensure it is evenly cooked.

∂ Stir in the cooked eggplant and cook for about 8 minutes over low heat, then turn off the heat but leave the pan on the stove to cool slightly and allow the flavors to meld. Serve warm with Eastern-Style Focaccia (*see* page 53) or toasted bread.

Yogurt with Cucumber, Garlic & Dill
Cacik

Pronounced "ja-jik," this yogurt dish is a staple when ordering grilled meat in any Turkish restaurant. Much like the Greek *tzatziki*, the addition of garlic sets it apart from India's raita and Iran's *maast o khiar*, but the dill is authentic to Turkey alone. Traditionally made with thick and creamy strained Turkish yogurt, I would suggest you find good-quality yogurt to ensure the best results, although no matter what you use, it will be the perfect pairing to rich grilled meat dishes.

SERVES 4 AS PART OF A MEZZE

1 large cucumber, coarsely grated or finely diced

generous 2 cups (500ml) Greek yogurt

1 fat garlic clove, crushed

1 x ¾oz/20g packet of dill, stalks and leaves finely chopped

sea salt and freshly ground black pepper

extra virgin olive oil, for drizzling

∂ Carefully squeeze out and discard the excess water from the grated cucumber—you can do this by hand or in a sieve. Place the cucumber in a mixing bowl and mix in the yogurt.

∂ Add the garlic and dill, mix well, and season to taste with sea salt and black pepper. Serve with a drizzle of extra virgin olive oil.

Marinated Feta

Bread and cheese (or *naan-o-paneer* in Persian) are the opener to any classic Persian meal. We usually pair them with fresh herbs, fresh walnuts, radishes, and scallions. I came up with this dish as an alternative to the classic version and it has become a firm favorite with my diners and friends alike. It's great in salads and the marinade makes a tasty salad dressing with just a little extra lemon juice. Or simply scoop up the chunks of feta with bread.

SERVES 6-8 AS PART OF A MEZZE

14oz (400g) feta cheese

2–2½ cups (500–600ml) olive oil (the quantity depends on the size of the dish used to marinate the cheese)

generous ¼ cup (75ml) garlic oil

zest of 2 lemons and juice of ½ lemon

sea salt

3 long banana shallots, peeled and thinly sliced

10–12 pickled chilies, thinly sliced (and 3 tbsp of the pickle brine)

2 x ¾oz/20g packets of cilantro, stalks and leaves finely chopped

∂ You probably have 2 blocks of feta. Cut each into chunks—I would suggest 12 per block, but do as you wish. Put the chunks into a shallow bowl or airtight container.

∂ Pour the olive oil, garlic oil, lemon zest and juice, and salt to taste into a mixing bowl. Add the shallots, pickled chilies, and cilantro and mix well to ensure all the aromatics are evenly distributed in the marinade. Pour the pickle brine into the bowl and mix well.

∂ Arrange the feta in your chosen container, leaving a little space between each cube. Pour over the marinade, shaking the container to ensure the marinade covers the feta. Cover with plastic wrap and leave to marinate for a minimum of 3 hours before serving. This dish stores well overnight but keep it in an airtight container in the refrigerator and consume within a few days.

∂ **Tip**
To replace the brine in the jar of pickled chilies you use—just add cold water to cover the remaining chilies and a couple of pinches of salt before resealing.

Smoked Eggplants with Garlic
Mirza Ghasemi

Persians love eggplants and, for me, they are the meat of the vegetable world. If I were to ever become a vegetarian, I'd quite happily gorge myself silly on them. Smoking eggplants allows the flesh to absorb a deep smokiness, giving incredible depth to a dish. Hailing from the Gilan province of northern Iran, *mirza ghasemi* features on the menus of Persian restaurants all around the world.

SERVES 6-8

6 large eggplants

vegetable or olive oil

2 garlic bulbs, cloves peeled, bashed, and thinly sliced

1 heaped tsp turmeric

6 large ripe tomatoes, quartered

4 tbsp tomato paste

1 tsp sugar

3 heaped tsp crushed sea salt flakes (less if using table salt)

3 medium free-range eggs, beaten

handful of broken walnut pieces, to garnish

∂ The most authentic way to prepare the eggplants is to blister them whole over an open flame (either on a barbecue or over a domestic gas burner) until blackened and the flesh has softened right through to the center. Alternatively, place them in a roasting pan and roast them whole in a preheated oven at 425°F/220°C for 40–45 minutes.

∂ Put a good drizzle of oil into a large frying pan over medium heat and slowly cook the garlic slices, ensuring you cook them through rather than simply browning them. If they start to brown too quickly, take the pan off the heat and allow the residual heat to cook them through, if necessary. Once the garlic begins to brown around the edges, stir in the turmeric. Add the tomatoes to the pan and cook for about 15–20 minutes, or until they break down and are cooked through, then turn off the heat and set the pan aside.

∂ Once cooked, score the eggplant skin from stalk to base and scoop out the flesh using a large spoon. Stir this into the garlic and tomatoes. Place the pan over medium-high heat and cook through for a few minutes, mashing a little as you go. Lastly, add the tomato paste, sugar, and sea salt, stir well, and cook for a further 6–8 minutes, stirring occasionally to prevent the mixture from burning.

∂ Make lots of little holes in the eggplant mixture and pour the beaten eggs straight into the pan, but do not stir in the egg. You want to ensure the eggs are cooking and solidifying before you incorporate them—they take about 6 minutes to become opaque. Once cooked, give the mixture one final stir and remove the pan from the heat. Leave the mixture to cool for 20 minutes—this dish is best served warm rather than piping hot. Garnish with walnut pieces and serve with Persian Flatbread (*see* page 55).

Yogurt, Cucumber & Mint
Maast O Khiar

For Iranians, this dish serves the purpose of cooling you down in the sweltering summers. As in Turkey, Greece, and India, a yogurt dish of this sort is a staple on the table during every family meal. Iranians love to vary the content, often using beets or spinach in place of the cucumber. In the height of summer, this dish is virtually treated as a soup, so perhaps it is Iran's answer to the Spanish gazpacho. It should be served chilled and, on the hottest of occasions, with ice cubes to help it stay cool.

SERVES 6 AS PART OF A MEZZE

1 large cucumber, coarsely grated

2 tsp dried mint

generous handful of golden raisins

generous 2 cups (500ml) Greek yogurt

sea salt and freshly ground black pepper

To serve

olive oil

chopped walnuts

finely chopped fresh mint leaves

dried edible rose petals

∂ Carefully squeeze out and discard the excess water from the grated cucumber—you can do this by hand or in a sieve. Put the drained cucumber pulp into a mixing bowl.

∂ Add the dried mint and golden raisins to the bowl, followed by the yogurt, and mix well. Season to taste with sea salt and black pepper. Cover with plastic wrap and chill in the refrigerator until ready to serve. To serve, drizzle with a little olive oil and scatter with chopped walnuts, finely chopped mint leaves, and dried rose petals.

∂ **Variation**

Try adding chopped fresh dill or mint, as well as walnut pieces for a different take on this dish.

Smoked Eggplant Salad
Batinjan al Rahib

Known as *batinjan al rahib* in the Arab world, this dish uses just a few ingredients but delivers a big impact. It is virtually identical to the Turkish *patlican* salad and it's a dish I cannot get enough of. I love it, everyone I have made it for loves it, and the use of smoked eggplants is what makes it so special. Simplicity rules in the Middle East and the humblest of dishes often make the biggest impression.

SERVES 6-8

4 large eggplants

½ red pepper, cored, deseeded, and finely diced

½ green pepper, cored, deseeded, and finely diced

4–5 tbsp olive oil

2 garlic cloves, peeled and crushed

juice of 1–1½ lemons

sea salt and freshly ground black pepper

1 small bunch of flat leaf parsley, leaves picked and roughly chopped

∂ Blister and char the eggplants whole over an open flame (either on a barbecue or over a domestic gas burner) until blackened and the flesh has softened right through to the center. Really blacken and char the skins until they are hardened and completely burned. Then place the eggplants on a heatproof surface or tray and allow to cool until they are just warm and you are able to handle them.

∂ Scoop out the flesh using a large spoon. Drain off any excess juices and roughly chop the flesh into smallish chunks. Place the flesh in a bowl along with the diced peppers and give the mixture a quick stir.

∂ Pour the olive oil into a small bowl, add the crushed garlic, lemon juice, and sea salt and black pepper to taste, and give the dressing a good mix until all the ingredients are evenly blended. Pour the dressing over the eggplants, add the parsley, and mix everything together one final time before serving with Persian Flatbread (*see* page 55).

Persian Herb Frittata
Kuku Sabzi

This lovely deeply green frittata is very popular among Persians. I prefer to bake it because it is less messy and greasy than the original fried version, but also because laziness always gets the better of me. There are several different versions of this egg dish, known as *kuku* in Iran—with potato, eggplant, and meat—but this is the most popular and the one I like the most. It is often cut up into little squares and served as canapés at cocktail parties. You can omit the walnuts and barberries but I love them both, not only for texture but also for a burst of berry sharpness in every mouthful.

SERVES 8 AS PART OF A MEZZE

2 x 4oz/100g packets of flat leaf parsley

2 x 4oz/100g packets of cilantro

2 x ¾oz/20g packets of dill

3 x ¾oz/20g packets of chives

2–3 tbsp olive oil

2 bunches of scallions, thinly sliced

2 tsp turmeric

8 medium free-range eggs

2 tbsp all-purpose flour

2 tbsp Greek yogurt

3 tsp baking powder

2 tbsp crushed sea salt flakes (less if using table salt)

freshly ground black pepper

3–4 heaped tbsp dried barberries

3½oz (100g) walnut pieces, chopped

∂ Preheat the oven to 350°F/180°C. Place a large pot to warm over medium heat.

∂ Finely chop all the herbs (if you are using a food processor, you might need to do this in 2 batches). Pour the olive oil into the warm pan and fry the herbs and scallions for a few minutes, then add the turmeric. Cook for a further 5 minutes, then place the herbs on a flat plate and allow to cool.

∂ Meanwhile, mix the eggs, flour, yogurt, baking powder, and sea salt and black pepper to taste until everything is well combined and smooth. Once the herb mixture has cooled enough that it is no longer piping hot, slowly add a couple of spoonfuls at a time to the egg mixture and stir well until well combined. Add in the barberries and walnuts and mix well once again.

∂ Select a large ovenproof or Pyrex dish and line the dish with parchment paper (this will enable you to remove the finished dish with greater ease). Pour in the egg-herb mixture, then bake for 35–40 minutes. To check if the frittata is cooked, insert a knife into the center. If it comes out clear of raw egg, the dish is done. If not, return it to the oven for a few minutes. Once cooked, allow to cool, then cut into squares to serve.

Hummus

Hummus... who doesn't love it? Although this recipe deviates from the authentic Lebanese version, it allows you to make a pretty great hummus at home with a little help from a food processor. I also make a great lemon and cilantro variation for when you are in need of something a little different or if, like me, you have friends and family who are hummus addicts, so you need to offer up more than one version of the good stuff.

SERVES 8

3 x 14oz/400g cans chickpeas
(reserve the liquid of 1¼ cans)

about 4 tbsp olive oil,
plus extra for drizzling

4 tbsp garlic oil

juice of 3 lemons

4 tbsp light tahini

2 tbsp sea salt flakes
(less if using table salt)

sprinkling of paprika, to garnish

∂ First you need to mash the chickpeas, which I prefer to do by hand to give them a nice rough texture but, admittedly, it is a labor of love —whizzing them in a food processor gives them the smooth texture that we are more accustomed to. Use the chickpea liquid, a little at a time, and some olive oil to help the process and achieve an even texture. Add the garlic oil, lemon juice, and tahini, followed by the bulk of the remaining olive oil and the sea salt. Mix (or blitz) thoroughly.

∂ Add another thin drizzle of olive oil until you reach your desired consistency. Check the flavor to adjust the seasoning and/or add more lemon juice as required. Serve with a gentle drizzle of olive oil on top and a light sprinkling of paprika (if using) for color.

∂ **Variation**

To make a Lemon & Cilantro Hummus, add ¾oz (20g) very finely chopped cilantro leaves and the juice of 1½ more lemons to the recipe above and mix well. Serve with a drizzle of olive oil and scatter over more chopped cilantro if desired.

Spicy Tomato & Pepper Dip
Ezme

Ezme is a wonderful Turkish dish made with the ripest of tomatoes, which give it a deep, sweet flavor that contrasts with the fiery kick of chilies and the acidity of the vinegar and pomegranate molasses. Everyone seems to have their own recipe—some are spicier or less acidic than others, but this is my favorite version to eat with *Cacik* (*see* page 15) and bread. It is a staple when eating Turkish food.

SERVES 4 AS A DIP

4 ripe tomatoes, finely chopped

1 onion, very finely chopped

1 red pepper, cored, deseeded, and very finely chopped

1 green pepper, cored, deseeded, and very finely chopped

2 red chilies, deseeded and finely chopped

1 x ¾oz/20g packet of flat leaf parsley, leaves picked and finely chopped

2 tsp sumac, plus extra to garnish

1 tsp pomegranate molasses

2 tsp red wine vinegar

4 tbsp extra virgin olive oil, plus extra for drizzling

1 tsp crushed sea salt flakes (less if using table salt)

freshly ground black pepper

∂ In all truthfulness, you could simply put all the ingredients into a food processor and blitz the whole thing together with great ease. If you do this, then start with the onion first and put in the tomatoes last but, whatever you do, pulse them—don't blitz them to a purée or you will end up with a soup! And if you choose this method, add the dressing components after the vegetables are finely chopped.

∂ To do things the old-fashioned and authentic way, chop the tomatoes, onion, peppers, chilies, and parsley by hand, then put them into a large bowl. Add the sumac, pomegranate molasses, vinegar, olive oil, and sea salt and black pepper to taste before giving everything a stir. Cover with plastic wrap and put it in the refrigerator for 15 minutes to allow the dressing to macerate the vegetables.

∂ Once ready to serve, arrange on a flat plate and flatten with a fork, drizzle with a little extra virgin olive oil, and sprinkle with a couple of pinches of sumac.

Turkish Feta Pastry Cigars
Sigara Börek Peynir

Börek are Turkish pastries filled with either cheese, cheese and spinach, or ground meat. They come in all shapes and sizes, but I do like making individual *sigara-* (cigar-) shaped ones because they are perfect for serving as finger food and look quite lovely among a good selection of other dishes on the table. I like to fill mine with feta cheese and a hint of dried mint, which adds a wonderful warmth to the filling and gives it that little something extra.

MAKES 24

olive oil

5½–7oz (150–200g) feta cheese

2 tsp dried mint

1 tbsp Greek yogurt

6 sheets (1 packet) of filo pastry

3 large free-range eggs, beaten

nigella seeds, to decorate

∂ Preheat the oven to 400°F/200°C. Line a baking sheet with parchment paper and brush it generously with olive oil, which will prevent the cooked *börek* from sticking to the paper.

∂ Crumble and mash the feta cheese into a small bowl with the dried mint and Greek yogurt until the mixture is evenly blended but not "wet"—you need it to be soft enough to mold as desired.

∂ On a clean work surface, take a sheet of filo pastry and cut it into quarters. Have your bowl of beaten eggs on hand. Place one-quarter of the pastry horizontally in front of you. Take a teaspoon of mixture, roll it into a sausage shape in your hands, and place it along the bottom edge of the pastry. Fold the bottom corners of the pastry up over the filling, then roll up the pastry from the bottom, tucking in the sides as you go. Dab your fingers into the beaten egg and seal all sides to prevent the filling from leaking out during cooking.

∂ Place the rolled *börek* onto the prepared baking sheet and repeat with the remaining pastry and filling. Brush the *börek* all over with the beaten egg and give each one a scattering of nigella seeds, then bake for about 20 minutes, or until they are golden brown. Serve immediately.

Salt Cod Fritters

Preserving fish is very common around the world. We usually use *mahi doodi*, a dried smoked fish that can be found hanging in every grocery shop in Iran, especially around the time of Persian New Year, when it is the main focus of the annual feast. Personally, I'm not a big fan of it, but I do like using salt cod at home for a variety of dishes. My favorite is this one, delicate little fritters that are packed full of flavor and are very similar to those of Spanish and Portuguese origin. They make a great salty snack with drinks or as mezze with friends. I can't stop eating them until they are all gone.

MAKES ABOUT 16 FRITTERS

1lb 2oz (500g) salt cod (or salted pollock, which is sometimes found in supermarkets instead)

1lb 2oz (500g) cold mashed potatoes

1 x ¾oz/20g packet of flat leaf parsley, leaves picked and finely chopped

1 x ¾oz/20g packet of dill, leaves and stalks finely chopped

1 x ¾oz/20g packet of chives, snipped or thinly sliced

2 large red chilies, finely chopped (with or without seeds)

1 bunch of scallions, thinly sliced

4 fat garlic cloves, finely chopped

zest of 2 unwaxed limes

1 tsp turmeric

1 tsp ground ginger

3 large free-range eggs

1 tsp crushed sea salt flakes (less if using table salt)

freshly ground black pepper

3 heaped tbsp all-purpose flour

1 tsp baking powder

3 cups (700ml) vegetable oil

lime wedges, to serve

∂ Soak the salt cod in plenty of cold water. I usually soak mine for a minimum of 4–6 hours, refreshing the water every couple of hours to get rid of the excess salt. Once done, drain and dry the fish fillets completely using some paper towel to absorb excess moisture.

∂ Put the mashed potato and salt cod into a large mixing bowl and break down the cod using a fork. Add the herbs, chilies, scallions, garlic, lime zest, and dry spices, followed by the eggs and sea salt and black pepper to taste, and, using a wooden spoon, mix well until everything is evenly combined. Add the flour and baking powder and stir again. Cover the bowl with plastic wrap and refrigerate the mixture for at least 1 hour to get it nice and cold.

∂ Put the oil in a large saucepan over medium-high heat and allow it to get nice and hot, but do not let it smoke. Test a tiny bit of the mixture in the oil—if the oil sizzles within a couple of seconds, it is ready to use. In batches, drop the mixture into the oil a spoonful at a time. Don't worry about the fritters being of uneven shapes, as this is perfectly fine. Fry the fritters for about 2–3 minutes, then turn them over and fry them for about 1 minute on the reverse side. Remove them using a slotted spoon and drain on a plate lined with paper towel. Repeat until all the fritters are cooked. Serve with lime wedges.

Pistachio & Feta Dip

I discovered this dip in a backstreet butcher's shop-cum-restaurant in Istanbul. Naturally, they wouldn't tell me what was in it, so I had to do the guesswork myself and came up with a surprisingly accurate version of it. It draws influences from the Balkan states and I just love the salty, nutty nature of it. A kick of chili rounds it off beautifully and makes it impossible to resist with hunks of pillowy bread.

SERVES 8

3½oz (100g) shelled pistachios

generous ¼ cup (75ml) olive oil

10½oz (300g) feta cheese

handful of dill, leaves picked and roughly chopped

2 handfuls of cilantro, leaves picked and roughly chopped

1 garlic clove, peeled and crushed

1 long red chili (of medium heat), roughly chopped

3 large tbsp Greek yogurt

zest of 1 lemon and juice of ½ lemon

sea salt

∂ Blitz the pistachios and oil in a food processor for 30 seconds. Add the feta, herbs, crushed garlic, chili, yogurt, and lemon zest and juice and blitz the ingredients for about 1 minute, or until the mixture has a nice rustic texture. Taste the dip and season with just a touch of sea salt, if desired. Remember that the feta is quite salty already, so you really won't need much salt to season the dip. Serve with Eastern-Style Foccacia (*see* page 53).

Safavid-Style Beef Pastries

I simply adore any pastry that is filled with meat. Pies, *empanadas*, *bastillas*, and *börek*—every nation has some form of meat-filled pastry and no wonder, as it is delicious and offers a meal in itself. The Safavid dynasty ruled the Persian Empire from 1501–1722 and again from 1729–1736 and was one of the most significant in Persian history. The Safavids were powerful and their hold extended to many nations, from Azerbaijan to Turkey. Food is always a matter of importance in the Middle East, especially when entertaining. Elaborate dishes were the order or the day, using expensive and rare ingredients and spices. These pastries are typical of the time, and many of the countries ruled by the former empire still have similar pastries as part of their modern cuisines.

MAKES 12

vegetable oil

7oz (200g) ground beef

½ tsp turmeric

½ tsp ground cumin

½ tsp paprika

¼ tsp ground cinnamon

couple of pinches of ground nutmeg

¼ tsp chili powder

1 tbsp dried edible rose petals

sea salt and freshly ground black pepper

1 small red onion, very finely chopped

small handful of flat leaf parsley, leaves picked and finely chopped

1 ready-rolled puff pastry sheet, about 14 x 9½in (35 x 24cm)

3 tbsp (40g) butter, melted

∂ Preheat a large frying pan over medium-high heat, drizzle a little oil into the pan, and fry the ground beef, keeping it moving constantly to prevent it stewing or cooking unevenly. Once the beef begins to change color, add all the spices along with the rose petals and mix well so that they are evenly incorporated. Now season with sea salt and black pepper and continue to fry the beef until the mixture becomes dry and there is no moisture remaining in the pan. Remove the beef mixture from the pan and allow it to cool.

∂ Preheat the oven to 425°F/220°C. Line a large baking sheet with parchment paper.

∂ Once the spiced meat mixture has cooled, stir in the onion and parsley and mix them in well.

∂ Cut the puff pastry sheet into 12 squares. Take a heaped tablespoon of the beef mixture and place it in the center of a pastry square, then fold the square into a triangle, tightly pressing the edges together to seal. Repeat until all the meat mixture is used up. Place the triangles of filled pastry straight onto the paper-lined baking sheet, spacing them about ¾in (2cm) apart. Brush the tops with the melted butter, then bake for 20 minutes, or until golden and puffed up.

Baked Eggs with Feta, Harissa, Tomato Sauce & Cilantro

Baked eggs is one of my all-time favorite breakfast dishes. There is no joy greater than that of plunging in a piece of bread and pulling it out coated in unctuous egg yolk and whatever else goes with the eggs. I like my eggs spicy. Chili provides a great way of kick-starting your metabolism in the morning and harissa is a versatile condiment to have in the house for quick dishes. Chunks of wonderfully salty, creamy feta provide the perfect match for harissa. This versatile breakfast dish has been relied on for many wonderful evening meals in my home.

SERVES 4

4 tbsp olive oil

5 garlic cloves, bashed and thinly sliced

3 large red onions, cut in half and sliced into ½in- (1cm-) thick half moons

2 tsp turmeric

1 tsp ground coriander

1 tsp ground cumin

½ tsp ground cinnamon

3 tbsp harissa

6 large tomatoes, roughly chopped

1 x 14oz/400g can chopped tomatoes

sea salt

2 x ¾oz/20g packets of cilantro, leaves picked and roughly chopped

14oz (400g) feta cheese

freshly ground black pepper

8 large free-range eggs

∂ To make the sauce, preheat a saucepan over medium heat and drizzle in just enough oil to lightly coat the base of the pan. Sauté the garlic slivers and onion slices until they begin to soften and become translucent. Add the turmeric, coriander, cumin, and cinnamon and stir well before adding the harissa paste. Put in the fresh and canned tomatoes, season generously with sea salt, and give everything a good stir, then reduce the temperature slightly and allow the sauce to cook for 15–20 minutes, stirring occasionally to prevent sticking.

∂ Preheat the oven to 350°F/180°C. Select a large baking dish (or 2 smaller dishes) and pour the spicy tomato sauce into it. Scatter the chopped cilantro onto the sauce (but save a handful for garnishing the finished dish) and give the mixture a very gentle stir to loosely incorporate the chopped leaves into the sauce. Break off 1in (2.5cm) chunks of the feta and dot them all around the dish, pushing some down under the sauce and leaving some on the surface. Make 8 evenly spaced craters in the surface and crack your eggs into them. Season the dish well with black pepper and another sprinkling of sea salt, then bake for 10–12 minutes, or until the whites of the eggs have turned opaque and are cooked through.

∂ Remove from the oven, sprinkle the last handful of chopped cilantro leaves over the dish and serve with bread. Persian Flatbread (*see* page 55) is ideal—you can scoop each mouthful straight out of the dish itself.

Spiced Beef & Potato Cakes
Kotlet

This recipe is one of the simplest elements of a Persian feast, which may explain why it is a staple at many family parties, particularly around the time of the Persian New Year. The best and most popular way to eat these patties is actually the day after your party, stuffed into some bread with slices of tomato and pickle. Either way, they are absolutely delicious and incredibly easy to make in large quantities. Feel free to adapt the recipe to your taste, substituting ground veal, lamb, chicken, or turkey for the beef.

MAKES ABOUT 12

4oz (115g) breadcrumbs, blitzed to a fine consistency in a food processor

1lb 2oz (500g) ground beef

1lb (400g) cooked potato, peeled, mashed, and cooled

1 onion, ground in a food processor or very finely chopped

1 x ¾oz/20g packet of cilantro, stalks and leaves finely chopped

2 free-range eggs

2 tsp garlic granules or 1 heaped tsp garlic powder

2 tsp ground cumin

1 tsp turmeric

½ tsp ground cinnamon

2 heaped tsp crushed sea salt flakes (less if using table salt)

freshly ground black pepper

vegetable oil

∂ Pour the breadcrumbs onto a flat plate, ready for coating the patties.

∂ Put the remaining ingredients, except for the oil, into a large mixing bowl and, using clean hands, mix thoroughly. You really need to employ your fingers and squelch through the mixture to ensure it is evenly combined and the egg and spices are evenly distributed.

∂ Preheat a large nonstick frying pan over medium-low heat if using gas, or medium heat if cooking on electric, and preheat the oven on a low setting.

∂ Take a ball of the mixture (slightly larger than a golf ball), roll it in between your palms, and flatten it into a patty shape. Lay the patty gently onto the breadcrumbs and coat each side with enough breadcrumbs to cover the surface on both sides. Set aside and repeat the process until all the patties are made and coated.

∂ Drizzle a little oil into the preheated frying pan and fry several patties at a time (without crowding the pan) for 6–8 minutes on each side, or until nicely browned. Carefully remove them and drain on a plate lined with paper towel, then transfer to the oven and keep the cooked batches warm while you fry the remaining patties. Serve either with Persian Flatbread (*see* page 55) or on their own.

Lahmacun

Often described as mini Turkish pizzas, these breads (pronounced "lah-ma-jun") are traditionally fired up in seconds in the searing heat of a wood-fired oven. Topped with spicy ground lamb and herbs, they are great as a snack or a main meal. For me, adding meat to anything can only improve it, so I'm a huge fan of *lahmacun*. Making them in your own home isn't a chore at all and you can achieve pretty spectacular results. This is great family food, although hold back on a little of the spicing if not everyone likes chili heat.

MAKES 8

For the dough

1 tsp sugar

2 x ¼oz/7g envelopes active dry yeast, dissolved in 2 tbsp warm water

2 cups (10½oz/300g) white bread flour

1 tsp crushed sea salt flakes (less if using table salt)

⅔ cup (150g) Greek yogurt

scant ¼ cup (50ml) olive oil, plus extra for brushing

For the topping

½lb (250g) ground lamb

2 ripe tomatoes, deseeded and finely diced

1 onion, finely chopped

2 tsp Turkish dried chili flakes (*Pul Biber*) or 2 red chili peppers, deseeded and finely chopped

handful of finely chopped flat leaf parsley leaves

sea salt and freshly ground black pepper

lemon wedges, to serve

∂ Add the sugar to the dissolved yeast and stir. Allow it to sit for about 10 minutes until it becomes frothy.

∂ Sift the flour into a large bowl, then add the sea salt. In a small bowl, combine the yogurt with the olive oil until evenly mixed. Make a well in the center of the flour and pour in the yogurt mixture, along with the yeast mixture. Using your hands, work the flour into the liquid until a dough forms, then work the dough into a smooth ball, adding flour or a little splash of water if needed.

∂ Knead the dough for 5 minutes, then allow it to rest for 10 minutes before kneading it again for 1 minute. Repeat this process another 3 times, then return the dough to the bowl, cover with a clean dish towel, and leave it to rest somewhere warm for a couple of hours until it doubles in size. Knock back the dough and divide it into 8 balls. Roll these out into roughly 6in- (15cm-) diameter circles and brush with olive oil.

∂ Preheat the oven to 425°F/220°C. Line 2 large baking sheets with parchment paper.

∂ To make the topping, put the lamb, tomatoes, onion, chili, parsley, and a generous amount of salt and pepper into a large mixing bowl and work the mixture really well, pushing the meat through your fingers to break down the fibers. Turn out the mixture onto a chopping board and, using a large knife, chop it for several minutes until it resembles a paste.

∂ Divide the topping into 8 portions and smear over each of the dough bases (you don't need to cover the dough entirely). Place each on the prepared baking sheets and bake for 10–15 minutes, or until the dough is cooked and the crust begins to turn golden. Serve immediately with lemon wedges.

Spiced Lamb *Kefta*

Kefta **means "to pummel" and every country in the Middle East seems to have its unique version. Whether Turkish *köfte*, Persian *koofteh*, or Arab *kefta* or *kofta*, each variation is absolutely delicious and uses ingredients typical of the cuisine of its own culture. This particular version features currants and pine nuts. I love this union because not only do you get a burst of juicy sweetness but also the satisfying crunch of toasted pine nuts, making it a winning combination for me. Serve these *kefta* with rice, naan bread, or soft tortilla wraps—and a dollop of thick Greek yogurt really complements them too.**

MAKES 14–16

1lb 2oz (500g) ground lamb (not too lean)

1 large onion, ground in a food processor or very finely chopped

1 heaped tsp turmeric

½ tsp ground cinnamon

2 heaped tsp ground cumin

1½ tbsp crushed sea salt flakes (less if using table salt)

1¾oz (50g) pine nuts, lightly toasted

large handful of currants

2 x ¾oz/20g packets of flat leaf parsley, leaves and stalks finely chopped

2 large free-range eggs, beaten

vegetable oil

∂ Preheat a large nonstick frying pan over medium heat. Preheat the oven to 300°F/140°C.

∂ Put all the ingredients, except for the oil, into a large mixing bowl. Using your hands, mix everything together. Really work the mixture for a good few minutes, taking the time to pummel the meat until it has broken down, and to ensure that the egg and spices are evenly distributed into the mixture.

∂ Take a handful of mixture slightly larger than a golf ball, and shape into small, elongated sausage-like *keftas*, just over 2in (5cm) long, with slightly pointed ends and fatter middles. This is the traditional *kefta* shape, but you could also shape them into patties or simply make meatballs— the choice is yours.

∂ Heat a drizzle of oil in the preheated frying pan over medium-high heat and fry the patties in batches, without crowding the pan. Don't flip the *kefta* over until you see a little brown crust forming on the underside. Brown on all sides, then transfer to an ovenproof dish lined with parchment paper and keep the cooked batches warm in the oven while you fry the remaining *kefta*.

∂ **Tip**
These cooked *kefta* can also be added to a slow-cooked spiced tomato sauce (such as the sauce on page 117), and served with rice or potatoes.

Spice Salted Squid

No matter what form of squid I have eaten—whether in curries, chargilled, stuffed, baked, or deep-fried—I adore the stuff. It is still relatively cheap to buy, especially when frozen, which is perfectly fine. I like to use the smaller squid tubes rather than the giant ones, which I find comparatively tough. In this dish, the squid is crunchy and delicious. The same cooking method and coating also works well with shrimp.

SERVES 4–6 AS PART OF A MEZZE

3 cups (700ml) vegetable oil, for frying

1lb 10oz (750g) baby squid (frozen works well)

2 tbsp black peppercorns

3 tbsp crushed sea salt flakes (less if using table salt)

3 tsp ground cumin

2 tsp ground coriander

1½ tsp turmeric

scant ½ cup (2½oz/70g) cornstarch

∂ Put the oil in a large, preferably slightly deep, frying pan (or even in a cooking pot, if you prefer) over high heat and allow it to get nice and hot, but do not let it smoke.

∂ Meanwhile, cut the squid tubes into rings—up to about ½in (1cm) thick is ideal—and leave the tentacles whole. Dry them as best as possible using a clean dish towel or paper towel and set aside.

∂ Using a mortar and pestle, crush the peppercorns as best you can, then add the sea salt and other spices and grind them until they are evenly combined. You don't need to make a fine powder of the spices, so don't worry about the odd chunk of broken peppercorn.

∂ Combine the cornstarch with the spice mixture in a plastic sandwich or freezer bag and give it a good shake to ensure the ingredients are evenly distributed. Add the squid and toss the coating lightly over it without excessively handling the squid itself (otherwise you will create a paste when the cornstarch combines with the juice of the squid, which you want to avoid).

∂ Shake off the excess coating from the squid pieces and fry them in batches, without crowding the pan too much. Cook each batch for about 1–1½ minutes, depending on the oil temperature, or until you can see them browning and becoming crisp. Using a slotted spoon, drain the squid on plates lined with paper towel and serve hot.

∂ **Variation**

To make a quick dip, stir some quince paste into a tub of store-bought aioli to give it a real Middle Eastern flavor.

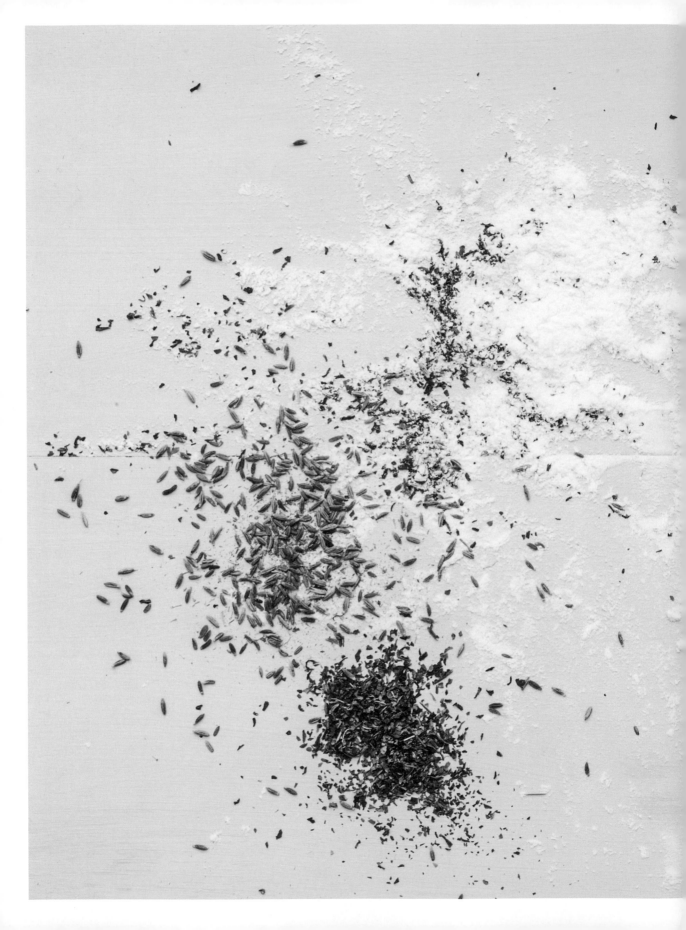

Breads & grains

Eastern-Style Focaccia

I love focaccia. Its pillowy texture and olive oil-soaked, salted crust give life to the idea of the humble loaf. When I master a baking recipe, I tend to experiment with adding ingredients and come up with a variety of versions. This Eastern-style focaccia was one of the successful trials and is great with salty cheeses or for livening up a humble bowl of soup. It also makes for fabulous sandwiches (with feta and roasted peppers, for instance) and provides a superb accompaniment to dips such as hummus and the like.

MAKES 1

½ cup (125g) cold sour cream

⅔ cup (150ml) cold water

scant ½ cup (100ml) boiling water

3 tsp sea salt flakes, crushed (less if using table salt), plus extra for topping

2 tsp superfine sugar

2 x ¼oz/7g envelopes active dry yeast

3½ cups (1lb 4oz/550g) white bread flour

3 tbsp cumin seeds

1 tbsp ground coriander

1 tbsp dried mint

1 tsp dried red chili flakes

generous ¾ cup (200ml) extra virgin olive oil

4 sprigs of thyme, leaves picked

1 tsp nigella seeds

1 tsp sumac

∂ Mix the sour cream with the cold and boiling water in a large bowl. Add the salt with the sugar and yeast, then blend in the flour, 2 tablespoons of the cumin seeds, the ground coriander, dried mint, and the chili flakes until the mixture forms a rough ball. Cover the bowl with plastic wrap and leave the dough to rest somewhere warm for 10 minutes to rise.

∂ Line a large roasting pan with some parchment paper and place the dough on top. Stretch out the dough to the size of your pan, then using your fingers, poke deep holes all over it. Try not to pierce the dough, but you can be pretty tough with it. Cover the pan with plastic wrap and leave the dough to rest somewhere warm for 1 hour (or longer, if you like).

∂ Once the hour is up, preheat the oven to 400°F/200°C. Remove the plastic wrap covering from the dough and drizzle the extra virgin olive oil over it, ensuring it covers every nook and cranny. A silicone brush will aid this process. Sprinkle the entire surface of the dough liberally with uncrushed sea salt flakes, thyme leaves, nigella seeds, the remaining cumin seeds, and the sumac. Place the baking sheet on the top shelf of the oven and bake for 25–30 minutes, or until golden brown.

Persian Flatbread
Naan Barbari

This bread has a lovely pillowy texture, with the added nuttiness of nigella seeds—perfect for dips and mopping up sauces. I'm often put off by bread recipes that require machinery, but expert baker Dan Lepard once gave me a tip for easy kneading which I now use to make almost all my breads, and they are always successful and wonderfully light.

MAKES 2 LARGE LOAVES

1 x ¼oz / 7g envelope active dry yeast

generous 2 cups (500ml) warm water

4½ cups (1½lb/700g) white bread flour

2 heaped tbsp crushed sea salt flakes (less if using table salt)

generous ¼ cup (75ml) olive oil

3½ tbsp (50g) butter, melted

nigella seeds, to scatter on top (or use sesame seeds)

∂ Stir the yeast into scant ¼ cup (50ml) of the warm water, then allow it to sit for a few minutes until it has dissolved.

∂ In a large bowl, combine the flour and sea salt, then make a well in the center. Pour in the remaining warm water, most of the of the olive oil (reserving about 2 tablespoons), and the yeast water and combine using your hands until you have a smooth dough. If the dough is a bit too sticky, just add a little extra flour and, if it is dry, an additional splash of warm water.

∂ On a clean, floured surface, knead the dough for 5 minutes to activate the yeast and stretch the glutens within it. Allow the dough to rest for 10 minutes before kneading it again for 2 minutes. Repeat this process another 3 times and, on the second, incorporate the remaining 2 tablespoons (25ml) or so olive oil. Return the dough to the bowl, cover it with a clean dish towel, and leave it to rest for 3 hours.

∂ Once the resting period is over, the dough will have tripled in size. Elongate the dough ball gently by stretching it from both ends, and then cut the dough in half. To form the correct shape for the bread, you will need to stretch each piece of dough into a long flat shape, about 16in (40cm) long. Place each shaped piece of dough on a baking sheet lined with parchment paper. Using a sharp knife or pizza cutter, make 2 lengthways incisions 2–3¼in (5–8cm) away from each end. Finally, cover each baking sheet with clean dish towels and leave the dough somewhere warm for a further 30 minutes to allow it to rise.

∂ Preheat the oven to 425°F/220°C. Once the loaves have risen, brush with the melted butter and sprinkle with nigella seeds. Bake for 16–18 minutes, or until golden brown. The best way to check if they are cooked through is to tap them with a spoon or knife—they should sound hollow. Allow to cool for at least 30 minutes before serving.

Persian Herb Rice
Sabzi Polow

This is a very special rice dish that, sadly, most Persians only eat once a year, at Persian New Year, which coincides with the spring equinox. It is fragrant and aromatic with an array of fresh herbs. As part of the New Year feast it is traditionally served with smoked dried fish, but any fish, such as salmon, cod, or smoked mackerel (our family favorite), works just as well. Even without fish, it is really delicious and my only advice to you is this—don't forget the butter! Butter really makes every rice dish so much better.

SERVES 4-6

2½ cups (1lb 2oz/500g) basmati rice

sea salt

1 x 4oz/100g packet of cilantro, leaves picked

1 x 4oz/100g packet of flat leaf parsley, leaves picked

2 x ¾oz/20g packets of chives

2 x ¾oz/20g packets of dill, leaves picked

1 x ¼lb/125g bunch of scallions

3 tbsp vegetable oil

10½ tbsp (150g) butter

∂ Wash the rice in cold water in a large bowl, then rinse and drain it. Repeat the process with more cold water until the water runs clear.

∂ Cover the rice with cold water, add a fistful of crumbled sea salt to the water, and allow the rice to soak for 2–3 hours. Soaking isn't compulsory, but even 30 minutes soaking time will help elongate the grains, making for a more elegant rice dish.

∂ If you don't have a food processor, finely slice the herbs and scallions. Don't worry about getting them too finely chopped, but do make an effort to chop them as best as you can. If you have a food processor, life is a whole lot easier because you can add all your herbs (in 2 batches) to the processor and pulse them until finely chopped. Give them a little chop first to make it easier for the processor to break them down. Chop the scallions into 4 or 5 pieces and blitz them in the processor, too, until finely sliced. Once done, add the herbs to the scallions and set aside.

∂ Preheat a cooking pot over medium heat if using gas, or medium-high heat if using electric. Fill the pan with boiling water, drain the rice, and add it to the pan along with another fistful of crumbled sea salt and the chopped herbs and scallions. Stir well and allow to boil for 6–8 minutes until the rice is parboiled (when the grains turn from the normal whiteish opaque to a more brilliant white, although they will not have become fluffy yet). Drain the rice and herbs in a colander and set aside (do not rinse).

∂ Return your cooking pot to the stove and pour in the oil with a couple of generous pats of the butter and 1 tablespoon crushed sea salt flakes (less if using table salt). Scatter the rice into the pan. Ensure you scatter it—don't pack it, because you want the lightness of the falling rice to allow for steam to rise up. Add the remaining butter. Wrap the pan lid in a dish towel (to lock in the steam and make for a secure, tight seal), cover the pan, and cook for 8 minutes on the same medium-high temperature. Then reduce the heat to low-medium and cook for a further 25–30 minutes.

∂ Once the rice is cooked, remove it from the pan (I like to place a large serving dish over the pan and flip the rice onto the dish), then scrape out the tasty *tahdig* (meaning "bottom of the pan"—this is the crusty bit every Persian fights over) and serve this on top of the rice.

∂ **Tip**

Line the pan with parchment paper to prevent the *tahdig* from sticking to the base of the pan. If you scrunch up or crush the paper before smoothing it out again, it makes it more malleable and easier to use to line the pan.

Persian Bejeweled Rice
Morassa Polow

Traditionally this dish is served at weddings. The word *morassa* literally means "jewel," reflecting the colorful ingredients. The slightly unconventional addition of sugar sweetens the rice (which counters the fiercely sour barberries and the tangy orange zest). This opulent dish epitomizes the Persian tradition for incorporating fruit and nuts into savory cooking.

SERVES 6

2½ cups (1lb 2oz/500g) basmati rice

3 tbsp vegetable oil

10½ tbsp (150g) salted butter

sea salt

1¾oz (50g) slivered pistachios

1¾oz (50g) slivered almonds

1¾oz (50g) dried barberries

1½oz (40g) dried, chopped sour orange peel (available from Middle Eastern shops)

scant ⅔ cup (4½oz/125g) superfine sugar

∂ Fill a large saucepan with boiling water and place over medium-high heat. Add the rice and boil for 8 minutes. Drain the rice and rinse it immediately under cold running water for a couple of minutes until it is cool, to wash off all the excess starch. Drain the rice again and shake off as much excess water as possible.

∂ Reduce the heat to the lowest setting. If your pan is not nonstick, line its base with parchment paper (*see* tip on page 59). Add 2 tablespoons of the oil and about one-third of the butter as well as a generous sprinkling of crushed sea salt, then gently scatter in the rice. Pile it up so that the rice forms a raised peak in the middle.

∂ Wrap the pan lid in a dish towel (to lock in the steam and make for a secure, tight seal), cover the pan, and cook the rice for around 1 hour. Because all stoves differ, check the rice during this time to see if all the grains right up to the very top are steamed, fluffy, and white. If the top grains look solid and opaque rather than fluffy and white, replace the lid and steam for longer. Once cooked, turn off the heat.

∂ Place a large frying pan over high heat, add the remaining butter and oil and all the nuts, barberries, orange peel, and sugar and stir thoroughly and quickly. Keep mixing until the sugar and butter have dissolved into the nut mixture, then reduce the heat to low and cook until the berries are soft but not colored.

∂ Once the rice is cooked, fill a large mixing bowl with two-thirds of the rice and stir in the nut-and-berry mixture. Carefully mix it through and season with salt as desired. The rice left at the bottom of the pan (*tahdig, see* page 59) will have a golden crust underneath, so peel away the parchment paper and enjoy!

Persian Basmati Rice
Chelo

Rice is the holy grail of Persian cuisine and the center of every meal; how well you cook your rice defines how good a cook you are. This method is one of the few in the world that does not cook rice by water absorption; instead the rice is steamed to achieve elegant, separated grains. The two most important elements to strive for when cooking rice are the length of grain and its perfume or natural aroma. Once tried, it is hard to cook rice by any other method. You might even pull off a crispy *tahdig* crust, but don't beat yourself up if not as it takes practice—and luck, at the best of times.

SERVES 6

2½ cups (1lb 2oz/500g) basmati rice

sea salt

light olive oil

4 tbsp (60g) butter

ᵟ Preheat a large saucepan over medium heat if using gas, or medium-high heat if using electric. Fill the pan with boiling water and add the rice with a handful of crumbled sea salt. Boil for 6–8 minutes until the rice is parboiled. You will know it is parboiled when the color of the grains turns from the normal dullish white to a more brilliant white and the grains become slightly elongated and begin to soften.

ᵟ Drain the rice and rinse it immediately under cold running water for a couple of minutes to wash off all the excess starch until it is cool. Line the bottom of the saucepan used to parboil the rice with some parchment paper (*see* tip on page 59).

ᵟ Return the paper-line saucepan to the stove and pour in a generous drizzle of oil with a couple of good pats of butter and about 1 tablespoon crushed sea salt flakes (less if using table salt). Now scatter the rice into the pan. Ensure you scatter it—don't pack it, because you want the lightness of the falling rice to allow for steam to rise up. Wrap the pan lid in a dish towel (to lock in the steam and make for a secure, tight seal), cover the pan, and cook the rice on the lowest temperature possible if using gas, or medium-low heat if using electric, for around 45 minutes on gas and up to 1½ hours on electric. The grains should be puffed up when cooked.

ᵟ To serve, either flip the rice onto a serving dish or decant onto a serving platter, then scrape out the crispy *tahdig* (*see* page 59) and serve it on top of the rice.

Rice with Lentils & Crispy Onions

Mojardara

Known as *mojardara* in Arab cuisine, versions of this rice dish appear in the cuisines of many countries. Growing up, the version we ate had no spicing but was abundant with lentils and raisins or dates. The Arab recipe has fried onions and, I must say, I do love fried onions, in anything, on anything, and with anything … in fact, I don't know many people who don't like fried onions. The nature of this dish is very simple and simple food is always what becomes most popular in its place of origin. All I would say is that I usually double this recipe because I like to eat it for several days afterwards, so keep that in mind when making yours.

SERVES 6–8

1⅔ cups (400ml) vegetable oil

4 large onions, cut in half and thinly sliced into half moons

1½ cups (10oz/275g) green lentils

1 tbsp cumin seeds

1½ cups (10½oz/300g) basmati rice

1 tsp ground coriander

2 tsp ground cumin

2 tsp ground cinnamon

1½ tsp turmeric

sea salt

2¼ cups (525ml) water

∂ **Variation**

For a fruity flavor, add a couple of handfuls of raisins to the lentils once drained.

∂ Pour the oil into a large saucepan and preheat it over high heat. Fry the onions (in 2–3 batches) for about 8 minutes, stirring once or twice, until golden brown and crispy. Remove them with a slotted spoon and drain on a plate lined with paper towel. Drain and discard the oil from the pan.

∂ Bring a large saucepan of water to a boil, add the lentils, and cook for about 15 minutes, or until they soften, but don't let them turn to mush. Drain and rinse them in cold water to stop them cooking any further.

∂ Put the pan you fried the onions in over medium heat, add the cumin seeds, and fry them for a minute or so before adding the rice, the other spices, and a generous amount of sea salt. Next, add the lentils (and raisins if using—*see* tip), and stir well. Add the water, give the mixture one last stir, then cover with a lid, reduce the temperature to the lowest setting, and cook for 20 minutes. Turn off the heat and leave to sit for 10 minutes with the lid on—this will allow the rice to cook through.

∂ Use a fork to separate the grains, then mix three-quarters of the fried onions into the rice. Serve on a platter with the remaining fried onions scattered on top.

Tomato Bulgar
Bulgur Pilavi

This is the most traditional staple served alongside Turkish kebabs. While we prefer rice in Iran, Turks prepare this simple but delicious tomato and bulgar dish, which I absolutely love either hot or cold, and even with or without kebabs, if I'm honest. Not only is it simple, it is cheap to make and is therefore popular all over Turkey.
I like to eat it with lots of *Cacik* (*see* page 15) on the side, and if there are any kebabs going, then that's a bonus.

SERVES 4

olive oil

1 large onion, finely chopped

1 red pepper, cored, deseeded, and finely diced

2 tbsp tomato paste

sea salt and freshly ground black pepper

generous 1 cup (7oz/200g) bulgar

generous pat of butter

generous 2 cups (500ml) water or chicken or vegetable stock

∂ Place a large nonstick saucepan over medium heat, drizzle in enough olive oil to coat the base of the pan, and soften the onions, stirring to prevent them from coloring too much. Add the diced pepper and stir for a further minute, then add the tomato paste and a generous amount of sea salt and black pepper. Now cook off the tomato paste for a few minutes, stirring to ensure the mixture doesn't burn. Add just a little more oil if you wish.

∂ Add the bulgar and butter to the pan, then pour in the water or stock and give the mixture a good stir until the tomato paste has dissolved into the liquid evenly. Cover the pan with a tight-fitting lid, reduce the heat to low-medium, and cook for 15–20 minutes, or until the water is fully absorbed. Once the bulgar is cooked, use a fork to fluff up the grains. Serve immediately.

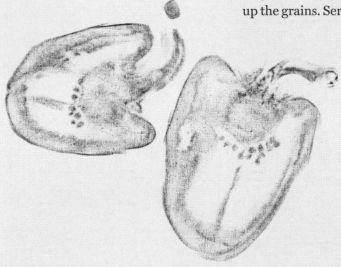

Spicy Shrimp Rice
Maygoo Polow

This spicy and totally delicious dish is based on a rice dish from the southern port of Bandar Abbas in Iran, and is not too dissimilar from a biryani. The spicing in this region is closer to that of the Arab states and Afghanistan, with a heavier use of spices and chili. If it has any kind of seafood in it, then it's a win-win situation as far as I'm concerned. This dish makes a great centerpiece on any dinner table and is a Sunday night favorite in my home. Although it's not that spicy, it is quite common to serve yogurt on the side for those who might need a little help in cooling their palate while eating this dish.

SERVES 6

2½ cups (1lb 2oz/500g) basmati rice

sea salt

vegetable oil

6 fat garlic cloves, bashed and thinly sliced

3in (7cm) piece of fresh root ginger, peeled and finely grated

1 tsp ground ginger

2 tsp ground cumin

1 heaped tsp dried fenugreek leaves

½ tsp ground cinnamon

½ tsp dried red chili flakes

1⅓ lb (600g) large raw peeled shrimp

freshly ground black pepper

4½ tbsp (60g) butter

∂ Preheat a large saucepan over medium-high heat. Fill the pan with boiling water and add the rice with a generous handful of crumbled sea salt. Boil for 6–8 minutes until the rice is parboiled. You will know it is parboiled when the color of the grains become a more brilliant white and the grains become slightly elongated and begin to soften.

∂ Drain the rice and rinse it immediately under cold running water for a couple of minutes until it is cool, to wash off all the excess starch. Line the bottom of the saucepan used to parboil the rice with some parchment paper (*see* tip on page 59) and set aside.

∂ Set a large frying pan over medium heat, drizzle in a generous amount of oil, and fry the garlic for about 30 seconds, then add the fresh and ground ginger, cumin, cinnamon, fenugreek leaves, and chili flakes and stir. Add the shrimp and cook them for less than a minute, or until their color begins to change to pink, then take the pan off the heat. Season well with sea salt and black pepper and stir the mixture one last time.

∂ Return the paper-lined saucepan to the stove and pour in a generous drizzle of oil along with the butter. Sprinkle in a couple of pinches of crushed sea salt, then scatter in just enough rice to cover the base of the pan with a good layer.

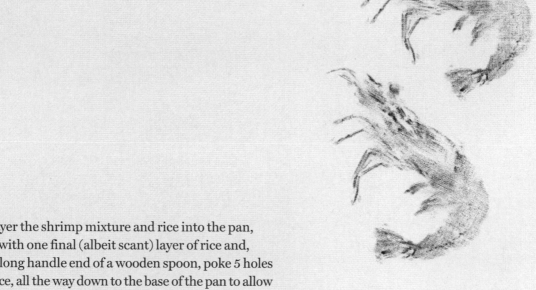

∂ Now layer the shrimp mixture and rice into the pan, finishing with one final (albeit scant) layer of rice and, using the long handle end of a wooden spoon, poke 5 holes into the rice, all the way down to the base of the pan to allow the steam to rise. Wrap the pan lid in a dish towel (to lock in the steam and make for a secure, tight seal), cover the pan, and cook the rice on the lowest temperature possible if using gas, or medium-low heat if using electric, for around 40 minutes.

∂ Once the rice is cooked, remove it from the pan (you can place a large serving dish over the pan and flip the rice onto the dish), then scrape out the crispy *tahdig* (*see* page 59) from the base of the pan and serve it on top of the rice.

Lamb Biryani

Biryani is a dish fit for a king and its origin is largely credited to Persia. The delicate layering of rice interspersed with spices and meat or poultry relies on a special Persian steaming method known as *dam pokht* (or *dum pukht* if you are from India), meaning "steam-cooked." There are now so many variations of biryani from India to Pakistan, but authentic versions have no chili pepper in them whatsoever—just aromatic spices such as luxurious Persian saffron. My wonderful friend Asma Khan is the Queen of Biryani and nobody has a more delicate and expert hand than she does when it comes to making the best and most authentic. Asma very kindly shared some of her biryani wisdom with me, from which I am delighted to share a simplified version of this hugely popular dish with you.

SERVES 6–8

1 cup (250ml) plus a few tbsp vegetable oil

6 large onions

1¾lb (800g) boneless lamb neck fillets, cut into 1in (2.5cm) chunks

1 tbsp green cardamom pods

6 black cardamom pods

4 bay leaves

2 tsp turmeric

2 tbsp cumin seeds

4 cinnamon sticks, each 3in (7cm) long

1 cup (200g) Greek yogurt

sea salt

3 cups (1lb 5oz/600g) basmati rice

2 generous pinches of saffron threads (optional)

2 tsp boiling water

9 tbsp (125g) butter

∂ Preheat a large saucepan over medium-high heat and pour in 1 cup (250ml) vegetable oil. Chop 4 of the onions in half, then thinly slice into ¼in- (5mm-) thick half moons. Fry the onion slices in the oil (there should be just enough oil to cover them, so add more oil if needed), stirring every few minutes, until they are golden brown and crispy. Using a slotted spoon, drain the onions onto a plate lined with paper towel and set aside.

∂ Pour out the oil, leaving behind just enough to coat the base of the pan. Roughly dice the remaining 2 onions and fry them over medium-high heat until they become translucent. Add the diced lamb and sear it until it begins to brown. Put in the green and black cardamom pods, bay leaves, turmeric, cumin seeds, and cinnamon sticks and mix well. Pour in just enough boiling water to barely cover the meat, reduce the heat to medium, and cook the lamb for about 1½ hours until just tender. Leave to cool. Once cooled, add the yogurt to the lamb, season generously with sea salt, stir well, and set aside.

∂ Preheat a large saucepan over medium-high heat. Fill the pan with boiling water and add the rice with a generous handful of crumbled sea salt. Boil for 6–8 minutes until the rice is parboiled. You will know it is parboiled when the color of the grains turns from the normal dullish white to a more brilliant white and the grains become slightly elongated and begin to soften.

∂ Drain the rice and rinse it immediately under cold running water for a couple of minutes until it is cool, to wash off all the excess starch. Line the bottom of the saucepan used to parboil the rice with some parchment paper (*see* tip on page 59) and set aside.

∂ Grind the saffron (if using) with a mortar and pestle, then pour over the 2 tablespoons of boiling water and leave to infuse.

∂ Back to the rice; return the paper-lined saucepan to the stove and pour in a generous drizzle of oil with a couple of good knobs of the butter. Add 1 tablespoon crushed sea salt flakes (less if using table salt). Scatter in just enough rice to cover the base of the pan with a good layer. Drizzle a little of the saffron water (if using) over this layer of rice. Take the yogurt-marinated pre-cooked lamb and divide it into two portions. Layer one portion over the rice, then cover with a thin layer of rice, sprinkle over some more saffron water (if using), then add a generous layer of crispy onions, and dot more butter on top. Repeat the layers until the rice, lamb, crispy onions, and butter are all used up.

∂ Wrap the pan lid in a dish towel, cover the pan, and cook the rice on the lowest temperature possible if using gas, or low-medium heat if using electric, for 30–45 minutes, or until the rice is cooked. When ready to serve, either flip the rice onto a serving dish or decant onto a serving platter, then scrape out the crispy *tahdig* (*see* page 59) from the base of the pan and serve it on top of the rice.

Soups, stews & tagines

Bamia

I think okra (or ladies fingers, as they are sometimes known) have managed to get a bit of a bad reputation over the years. Popular in Afro-Caribbean, Indian, and Middle Eastern cuisine, okra is often over-cooked or cooked without any added flavorings, resulting in a bland, slimy mess of a dish. But I grew up eating it in a spiced tomato stew with whole, melting garlic cloves and chunks of soft, slow-cooked meat, piled over steamed rice. I love the stuff. What's not to love? Cooked correctly, okra is absolutely delicious, and although Persians add meat to this dish, Arabs and Turks prepare the dish without, so it's an all-around winner.

SERVES 8

olive oil

2¼lb (1kg) lamb neck fillets, cut into 1in- (2.5cm-) thick slices (optional)

2¼lb (1kg) tomatoes, halved and cored

2–3 garlic bulbs, cloves bashed, peeled, and thinly sliced

5 tsp ground cumin

2 tsp ground cinnamon

4 tsp crushed sea salt flakes (less if using table salt)

2 tsp superfine sugar

2 x 14oz/400g cans chopped tomatoes

1½lb (700g) whole okra (the smaller, the better; frozen work well)

∂ Preheat a large, deep saucepan over medium heat and put in enough olive oil to generously coat the base of the pan. If using lamb, place the slices into the pan and lightly seal and brown them on the outside first (this will take roughly 8 minutes per side), then remove the slices from the pan and set aside.

∂ Firmly squeeze the halved tomatoes and arrange them in the pan, cut-side down. Add the garlic and shake the pan a little, then cook for 6–8 minutes, or until the tomatoes are soft and have separated from their skins. Give the mixture a good stir, then add the spices, sea salt, and sugar and give it a good stir again. Cook for a further 5 minutes, then add the chopped tomatoes and a little more olive oil. Stir again, reduce the heat to low, and return the lamb pieces to the pan (if using). Cover the pan with a lid and allow the contents to simmer for 1½ hours, stirring every 20 minutes or so to prevent sticking.

∂ After the cooking time has elapsed, taste the sauce and adjust the salt levels if required. Add the okra to the pan, stir gently to ensure each okra pod is covered in a little bit of sauce, then cook for a further 30 minutes with the lid off, stirring the okra pods gently from time to time to ensure they cook evenly. Serve with rice.

Spiced Vegetable Soup

This dish is more than just a simple broth—it is a wonderfully hearty meal and offers a great way of using up vegetables. There are no rules when making it; the simple truth is that this soup should contain whatever you might find lying around the house and in your fridge.

SERVES 4

olive oil

1lb 10oz (750g) peeled, deseeded butternut squash, cut into 1½in (4cm) chunks

2 large or 3 small onions, diced, plus 1 large onion, cut in half and thinly sliced into half moons

3 fat garlic cloves, crushed

3 leeks, trimmed, cleaned, and finely chopped

3 potatoes, unpeeled, cut into 1½in (4cm) rough chunks

5 ripe vine tomatoes, roughly chopped into chunks

4 heaped tsp ground cumin

1 heaped tsp ground cinnamon

2 tsp smoked sweet paprika

3 tsp hot pepper paste

sea salt and freshly ground black pepper

2 x 14oz/400g cans chickpeas (reserve the liquid, plus a couple of handfuls of chickpeas to garnish)

1 large zucchini, finely diced

3½oz (100g) feta cheese

For the Herb Oil

6 tbsp olive oil

good handful of flat leaf parsley

good handful of dill

good handful of cilantro

handful of shelled pistachios

squeeze of lemon juice

∂ Preheat a large saucepan over medium heat and add enough olive oil to generously coat the base of the pan. Add the butternut squash, diced onions, garlic, leeks, and potatoes and sauté, without browning, until the vegetables soften slightly. Then add the tomatoes, spices, and hot pepper paste and give it all a good stir to ensure the spices evenly coat the vegetables. Cover the vegetables completely with freshly boiled water, add a generous amount of sea salt (I would suggest at least 4 heaped teaspoons, crushed, a bit less if using table salt) and black pepper, stir once more, and allow to cook for 30 minutes on a gentle boil.

∂ Insert a knife into the squash and, when it is soft, purée the mixture in a food processor or blender until you get a lovely even, smooth soup. Once smooth, add the chickpeas and their liquid and stir well. At this stage you can add some more water to achieve your desired soup consistency, and check the seasoning to see if more salt or pepper is needed. Cook for a further 20 minutes, then add the zucchini and cook for a final 20 minutes before serving.

∂ Meanwhile, drizzle some olive oil into in a large frying pan set on high heat and fry the sliced onion until brown and crispy. Add the reserved chickpeas and brown them along with the onions. Using a slotted spoon, remove the onions and chickpeas from the pan and set aside.

∂ To make the herb oil, put the olive oil, parsley, dill, and cilantro in a bowl along with the pistachios, lemon juice, and some sea salt and pepper and blitz with a hand blender until it is finely chopped and has the consistency of pesto. If you need to slacken the mixture, add a bit more oil.

∂ Pour the soup into large bowls (preferably wide, shallow ones), then generously crumble the feta into the bowls. Drizzle a couple of tablespoons of the herb oil into each bowl over the feta. Finally, add the reserved crispy fried onions and chickpeas. Serve with some nice crusty bread.

Chicken, Preserved Lemon & Olive Tagine

This has to be one of the most classic tagine recipes of all time. A tagine (also the name of the conical earthenware dish in which these stews are traditionally cooked) is usually made with a combination of meat, poultry, or vegetables with spices, aromatics, and sometimes fruit and nuts. Although I do own a tagine dish, I find it more practical to make tagines in a conventional saucepan, which works in much the same way. I love the sharp, salty nature of this particular combination, and I could happily eat olives every single day for the rest of my life, which is why this tagine is made over and over again in my home.

SERVES 4–6

olive oil

3½ tbsp (50g) butter

2 large onions, roughly diced

4 large garlic cloves, thinly sliced

1 tsp ground coriander

1 tsp ground ginger

8 large bone-in chicken thighs, skin removed

pinch of saffron threads

2 tsp boiling water

sea salt and freshly ground black pepper

7oz (200g) green olives, pitted

6 preserved lemons, halved or sliced

1 x ¾oz/20g packet of flat leaf parsley, leaves picked and roughly chopped

∂ Heat a good drizzle of olive oil with the butter in a large saucepan set over medium heat. Add the onions and fry for a couple of minutes, then add the garlic slices and dry spices and mix well. Put in the chicken thighs and cook them for about 5 minutes on each side to seal them.

∂ Grind the saffron with a mortar and pestle, then pour over the boiling water and leave to infuse for a minute or two. Add the saffron water to the chicken and season with a generous amount of sea salt and black pepper. Pour in just enough water to barely cover the thighs, cover the pan with a lid, and cook for 2 hours.

∂ After the cooking time has elapsed, add the olives and preserved lemon slices and stir, then cover and cook for a further 15 minutes. Remove the tagine from the heat, add the roughly chopped parsley, and serve. Traditionally, tagine is not served with couscous, but of course you can serve it with couscous, rice, potatoes, or bread.

∂ **Tip**
To make homemade preserved lemons, take 10–15 small unwaxed lemons and scrub them clean. Cut them in half or into thick slices and pack them tightly into sealable sterilized jars with ½lb (250g) sea salt. Add a final layer of salt on top and seal the jars. Leave in a cool dark place for 3 months, turning every day. Ensure there is always a layer of salt at the bottom of the jar, and add more if necessary. The lemons will turn yellowish brown when ready to use. Once open, store in the refrigerator and cover with olive oil after each use.

Persian Saffron Chicken, Fennel & Barberry Stew

While fennel isn't a vegetable we use traditionally in Persian stews, I love the taste of it in this dish, since it absorbs the delicate chicken stock, perfumed with saffron, and it sweetens and mellows the flavor. For me, chicken in a stew must always be on the bone because that's where the flavor is. If you cook chicken thighs long enough, the fat melts away and the meat falls off the bone, so it is easy enough to discard the bones before serving if you prefer. This particular stew is a wonderful combination of gentle sweetness with little bursts of sharp sourness from the barberries.

SERVES 4–6

olive oil

2 large onions or 3 small onions, roughly diced

8 large bone-in chicken thighs, skin removed

generous pinch of saffron threads

2 heaped tsp ground cumin

½ tsp ground cinnamon

juice of 2 oranges

sea salt and freshly ground black pepper

2 large fennel bulbs, ends trimmed off, and cut into quarters

3 tbsp runny honey

2 large handfuls of dried barberries

∂ Set a large saucepan over medium heat if using gas, or medium-high heat if cooking on electric, and add a couple of good glugs (about 4 tablespoons) of olive oil to the pan. Fry the onions until they are translucent and just begin to take on a golden-brown color around the edges. Add the chicken thighs and coat them in the onion mixture to seal the flavor into the meat. Cook until you get just a little color onto the thighs.

∂ Grind the saffron with a mortar and pestle (or with your fingers when sprinkling it into the pot) and add it to the chicken, stirring well to ensure the chicken thighs are evenly coated in onion and saffron. Lastly, add the cumin, cinnamon, orange juice, and a generous amount of sea salt and black pepper and give everything a final stir.

∂ Pour over just enough boiling water to cover the chicken, then add the fennel quarters and honey. Cover the pan with a lid, reduce the temperature to low, and simmer for 1 hour, stirring after 30 minutes or so to prevent sticking. After the hour has passed, add the barberries and stir gently, then cover and cook for another hour. The slower and longer you cook this dish, the richer and better it will taste.

∂ After the full 2 hours of cooking, check the chicken and fennel to ensure they are still intact and give the ingredients another careful stir. Re-cover and cook for a further 20 minutes, then serve with basmati rice.

Chicken, Walnut & Pomegranate Stew
Khoresh-e-Fesenjan

Khoresh is the Persian word for stew. *Fesenjan* is a rich, glossy stew of ground walnuts and pomegranate syrup, usually made with chicken, duck, or delicate little lamb meatballs. The flavor is deep and rich, with a nutty texture and a wonderfully gentle acidity that cuts right through the richness of the dish. *Fesenjan* is a highly popular dish from Iran and its sweet yet tart character has made it one of the most revered stews in our repertoire. Like most stews, it's best made the day before you need to serve it.

SERVES 6–8

vegetable oil

2 large onions, diced

1 tbsp all-purpose flour

1lb 5oz (600g) walnuts, finely ground in a food processor

8 bone-in chicken thighs, skin removed

sea salt and freshly ground black pepper

5 cups (scant 1¼ liters) cold water

3 tbsp superfine sugar

2 cups (450ml) pomegranate molasses

seeds from 1 pomegranate, to serve

∂ Preheat two large saucepans over medium heat and pour 3 tablespoons vegetable oil into one. Fry the onions in the oil until translucent and lightly browned.

∂ In the other pan, toast the flour until it turns pale beige. Add the ground walnuts and cook the mixture through.

∂ Once the onions are browned, season the chicken on both sides with salt and pepper and add them to the pan containing the onions. Increase the temperature and stir well to ensure you seal the thighs on both sides. Once they are gently browned, turn off the heat and set aside.

∂ Add the water to the walnut pan, stir well, and bring the mixture to a slow boil, then cover with a lid and allow to cook for 1 hour over low-medium heat. This will cook the walnuts and soften their texture; once you see the natural oils of the walnuts rise to the surface, the mixture is cooked.

∂ Add the sugar and pomegranate molasses to the walnuts and stir well for about 1 minute. Take your time to stir the pomegranate molasses well—it takes a while to fully dissolve into the stew due to its thick consistency. Once this is done, add the chicken and onions to the walnut-pomegranate mixture, cover, and cook for about 2 hours, stirring thoroughly every 30 minutes to ensure you lift the walnuts from the bottom of the pan so that they don't burn. Once cooked, what initially looked beige will now have turned into a rich, dark, almost chocolaty-looking color. Serve sprinkled with pomegranate seeds and enjoy with a generous mound of basmati rice.

Lamb & Vegetable Tagine

This delicious lamb tagine is not only rich with meat but also brimming with vegetables, which balance an otherwise heavy meat dish perfectly. In Moroccan culture, vegetables are every bit as valued as meat, and this particular dish is a meal in itself and can be eaten without any accompaniment. The lamb shoulder cut imparts masses of flavor to the dish through its high fat content and, with slow cooking, the meat is so tender it simply falls apart. I love mashing the vegetables on my plate and spooning the juices on to them … it's the most decadent thing ever.

SERVES 6

olive oil

1 large onion, roughly diced

2 tsp ground ginger

2 tsp cumin seeds

2 tsp turmeric

½ tsp ground nutmeg

½ tsp cayenne pepper

½ tsp cubeb pepper

2¼lb (1kg) boneless lamb shoulder, diced into 8–10 pieces

pinch of saffron threads

2 tbsp boiling water

sea salt and freshly ground black pepper

6 small turnips, peeled and quartered

6 carrots, each cut into 3

8–10 shallots, peeled but kept whole

5 zucchinis, each cut into 3

argan oil

∂ Set a large saucepan over medium heat, add a good drizzle of olive oil, and fry the onion for a couple of minutes. Add all the dry spices except the saffon, then add the chunks of lamb and seal them for 5–6 minutes on each side to give them just a tiny bit of color.

∂ Grind the saffron with a mortar and pestle, then pour over the boiling water and leave to infuse for a minute or two. Add the saffron water to the pan and season with a generous amount of sea salt and black pepper. Add just enough water to barely cover the meat, place the lid on the pan, and cook over low-medium heat for 3 hours.

∂ After the cooking time has elapsed, add the turnips, carrots, and shallots and push them down slightly to semi-submerge them in liquid. Add more water if needed (but ensure you only add enough to just barely cover the contents), then re-cover and cook for another 45 minutes.

∂ Place the zucchinis gently on top of the tagine contents (ensuring they are not submerged), re-cover, and cook for a further 30 minutes until the zucchinis are just tender. Arrange the tagine on a large platter, drizzle with nutty argan oil, and serve immediately with couscous, rice, potatoes, or bread, or just enjoy it by itself.

Lamb Shank, Black Garlic & Tomato Tagine

As soon as I was introduced to black garlic at my very first supper club, I fell in love with its wonderfully sweet dark cloves. Black garlic is just normal garlic that has been slow-cooked in the oven for a long time until the cloves become deeply caramelized and jet black but without being burned, making them intensely sweet, soft, and delicious. You can eat them as is (which is my habit) or use them in cooking—they add a rich depth to a dish unlike any other ingredient. This dish is a real dinner party tagine and is very much my own recipe. I like serving it with sweet potato mash.

SERVES 6

olive oil

2 large onions, roughly diced

3 tsp ground cumin

2 tsp turmeric

1 tsp ground cinnamon

6 lamb shanks

sea salt and freshly ground black pepper

2 bay leaves

2 sprigs of thyme

2 x 14oz/400g cans chopped tomatoes

6 large tomatoes, halved

4 tbsp syrupy balsamic vinegar

2 black garlic bulbs, cloves peeled

∂ Set a large saucepan over medium heat and add a good drizzle of olive oil. Fry the onions for a couple of minutes, then add the dry spices, followed by the lamb shanks, and stir well. Seal the shanks on all sides until lightly browned, then fold the onion-and-spice mixture over them again and season well with sea salt and black pepper. Add the bay leaves, thyme, canned and fresh tomatoes, and balsamic vinegar, then pour in just enough water to cover the meat. Reduce the heat to low-medium, place the lid on the saucepan, and cook for 2 hours, stirring every 30 minutes to prevent sticking.

∂ Once cooked, add the soft black garlic cloves, plunging them into the sauce. Add a little more water to the pan if needed. Taste the tagine and adjust the seasoning, if desired, then cook the shanks for a further hour without the lid on before serving.

Persian Dried Lime, Lamb & Split Pea Stew
Khoresh-e-Gheymeh

Known as *khoresh-e-gheymeh*, this is one of the most popular stews of Iran and the great news is that it is one of the simplest to make. This is a great stew for people who have not yet tried Persian food, since the tomato base makes it a little more familiar than some of our other authentic stews. Its unique element is the wonderful sharpness imparted from the Persian dried Omani limes. Another variation adds eggplants, as fried halves or thick slices, and lastly, you can garnish the dish with thinly sliced fried potatoes … yes, like French fries. Sounds weird, but they're delicious on top of the finished dish.

SERVES 6–8

3 tbsp olive oil

3 small or 2 large onions, roughly diced

2¼lb (1kg) boneless lamb neck fillets, sliced into 1in (2.5cm) pieces

2 heaped tsp turmeric

2 generous pinches of saffron threads

1 heaped tsp ground cinnamon

5¼oz (150g) tomato paste

sea salt and freshly ground black peper

8 Persian whole dried limes (find Omani limes in Iranian and Middle Eastern supermarkets; sometimes called black limes) or preserved lemons

1 cup (7oz/200g) dried yellow split peas

∂ Set a large heavy-based saucepan over medium heat, add the olive oil and diced onions, and cook until the onions are softened, translucent, and cooked through. Increase the temperature to high, add the lamb, and fry the meat for about 5 minutes, stirring constantly to keep it moving and avoid stewing it.

∂ Stir the turmeric into the mixture until it evenly coats the meat. Do the same with the saffron and cinnamon, then add the tomato paste and a generous seasoning of sea salt and black pepper, give the meat a good stir, and cook for 1 minute.

∂ Prick your dried limes several times with a fork, then add them to the meat. Add just enough cold water to barely cover the contents of the pan. Stir well, then reduce the heat to very low and slow cook the stew for 1½ hours. Add the yellow split peas, check the seasoning, and cook for a further 1 hour. Serve the stew with basmati rice.

∂ Tip

This stew tastes even better the following day when, as we Iranians say, *jaa oftadeh*, which literally means "it has fallen into place," and the flavors have really united in a rich, thick sauce. The only problem is, you may not be able to wait that long! If you do manage to wait, stir in a little boiling water as you reheat the stew to revive the sauce content. But don't go overboard or it will thin out the flavor—a mug of hot water is all you need.

Spiced Lamb & Apricot Stew

Persian stews can be made with absolutely any combination of meat or poultry married with any available vegetable, or even fruit. Combining meat and fruit is a very Persian thing and this influence has most famously extended to both Indian and North African cuisines. When I make it, I've noticed that anyone who is with me while I cook is likely to ask me if perhaps I am being heavy-handed in my use of spices. But then, as if by magic, it all melds together to make a perfectly balanced aromatic stew with mouthfuls of plumped and revitalized dried apricots that taste as if they were fresh once again.

SERVES 6

vegetable oil

2 large onions, roughly diced

1½lb–1¾lb (600–800g) lamb neck fillets (or use diced, boneless leg, or 6 lamb shanks), cut into 1in- (2.5cm-) thick chunks

2 heaped tsp ground cumin

1 heaped tsp ground cinnamon

1 heaped tsp turmeric

sea salt

2 generous tbsp runny honey

½lb (250g) dried apricots

∂ Preheat a large saucepan over medium heat if using gas, or medium-high heat if cooking on electric. Drizzle in enough oil to cover the base of the pan, then add the onions and sauté them until they begin to brown slightly around the edges. Add the lamb to the pan and stir the meat into the onions, ensuring you keep the meat moving, so that it becomes nicely browned but does not stew.

∂ Add the spices to the pan, season with sea salt, and stir to coat the meat well, then add the honey and stir again. Pour in just enough boiling water to cover the ingredients, reduce the temperature to low, and simmer for 1¼ hours, stirring every so often to prevent sticking.

∂ After the cooking time has elapsed, add the apricots, stir well, and cook for at least a further 45 minutes. Serve with either basmati rice or Persian Flatbread (*see* page 55).

Lamb, Butternut Squash, Prune & Tamarind Tagine

This stew draws a lot of influence from the Persian Empire, from which the tradition of combining meat and poultry with fruit and nuts derives. It is fabulously spiced, and conjures up all the aromas of a souk or spice bazaar.

SERVES 6

vegetable oil

2 onions, roughly diced

1½lb–1¾lb (600–800g) lamb neck (or used diced, boneless leg or 6 lamb shanks), cut into 1½in (4cm) chunks

2 heaped tsp ground cumin

1 heaped tsp ground cinnamon

1 heaped tsp turmeric

sea salt

2 tbsp tamarind paste

2 heaped tbsp runny honey

1 small butternut squash, peeled, deseeded, and cut into 2in (5cm) chunks

2 generous handfuls of pitted prunes

∂ Preheat a large saucepan over medium heat if using gas, or medium-high heat if cooking on electric. Drizzle in enough oil to cover the base of the pan, then add the onions and sauté them until they begin to brown slightly around the edges. Add the lamb to the pan and stir the meat into the onions, ensuring you keep the meat moving so that it becomes nicely browned but does not stew.

∂ Add the spices to the pan with a generous seasoning of salt and stir well to coat the meat thoroughly, then stir in the tamarind paste and honey. Pour in just enough boiling water to cover the contents of the pan, reduce the temperature to low if using gas, or medium if cooking on electric, and simmer for 1½ hours, stirring every so often to prevent sticking.

∂ After the cooking time has elapsed, add in the chunks of butternut squash, stir well, and top up with a little more boiling water to just cover the contents of the pan. Cook for 30 minutes, then add your prunes, check the seasoning, and add more salt if necessary and cook for a further 30 minutes. Serve with basmati rice or Persian Flatbread (*see* page 55).

Pomegranate Soup with Meatballs
Ash-e Anar

This is one of my family's favorite soups. In fact, it's more hearty than a soup—it is more of a meal in itself. You can, of course, omit the meatballs entirely and opt for a vegetarian version. It's made both ways in Iran and both are equally delicious, but the most common way to eat it among Persians is with meat, because we do love a good meatball!

SERVES 4

olive oil

3 large onions, 2 roughly diced and 1 grated or ground in a food processor

4 fat garlic cloves, peeled and crushed

scant ½ cup (3oz/85g) dried yellow split peas

8½ cups (2 liters) water

1 heaped tsp crushed sea salt flakes (less if using table salt), plus a little extra for the meatballs

½ tsp freshly ground black pepper, plus a little extra for the meatballs

1 tsp turmeric

1 large bunch of parsley, leaves and stalks roughly chopped

1 large bunch of cilantro, leaves and stalks roughly chopped

1 small bunch of mint, leaves roughly chopped

3 small bunches of chives, roughly chopped

1lb (400g) ground lamb (ground beef and veal are also commonly used)

scant ½ cup (3oz/85g) basmati rice

1⅔ cups (400ml) pomegranate juice

3 tbsp pomegranate molasses

generous ½ cup (4½oz/125g) superfine sugar

∂ Preheat a large cooking pot over low-medium heat and drizzle in some oil. Add the 2 roughly diced onions and caramelize them. As they start to turn golden, add the garlic and brown gently with the onions. Put in the yellow split peas, pour over the water, and bring to a boil. Reduce the heat, partially cover the pan, and leave to simmer for 30 minutes over medium heat.

∂ Add the sea salt and black pepper, turmeric, and all the herbs and cook for a further 20 minutes, stirring to prevent the mixture from sticking to the bottom of the pan.

∂ To make your meatballs, combine the meat with the ground or grated onion and season generously with some salt and pepper. Roll the mixture into little meatballs about 1½in (4cm) in diameter. Add these to the soup pot along with the uncooked basmati rice, cover, and simmer for 30 minutes.

∂ Add the pomegranate juice, pomegranate molasses, and sugar and stir the mixture well, then half cover the pan with a lid and simmer for a further 30 minutes. Once cooked, you can adjust the thickness of the soup by adding more hot water, if desired, and also adjust the sugar and pomegranate molasses levels to your taste.

∂ **Tip**

To serve in the traditional manner, garnish the soup with caramelized onion slivers and dried mint. Fresh pomegranate seeds, chopped parsley, and cilantro are also delicious.

Seafood & Saffron Stew

This dish really reminds me of summer. I'm not really sure why, but I tend to make it when I need a little cheering up on a cold day. Seafood is a bit of a luxury these days, but a little goes a long way in this recipe and the sauce itself is incredibly simple and easy to make, so this is a great dish for entertaining. Not only does it look pretty spectacular but it delivers on the taste front, too. It has just a gentle chili kick that really satisfies. And the best part? Mopping up all the sauce with a big hunk of crusty bread. Absolute heaven.

SERVES 4

1¾lb (800g) mussels in their shells

scant 1lb (400g) small clams in their shells

4 tbsp olive oil

4 long French shallots, halved lengthways and thinly sliced into half moons

1 garlic bulb, cloves peeled and bashed (but not crushed)

good pinch of red pepper flakes

2 generous pinches of saffron threads, ground with a mortar and pestle

2 tsp turmeric

2 heaped tsp crushed sea salt flakes (less if using table salt), plus extra for soaking

freshly ground black pepper

1½lb (700g) passata or tomato purée

1 x 14oz/400g can good-quality tomatoes

2 tsp superfine sugar

12 raw shrimp (shell on or off)

½lb (200g) baby squid, cut into ½in (1cm) rings

8 scallops, roe discarded

large bunch of flat leaf parsley, leaves picked and finely chopped

squeeze of lemon juice

∂ Soak the mussels and clams in a big bowl of cold water with lots of sea salt in it. This will trick them into believing they are in the sea and they will open and close, expelling any sand or grit out of their shells into the water.

∂ Preheat the biggest saucepan you can find over medium-high heat, add the olive oil, and sauté the shallots for a few minutes, then add the garlic and red pepper flakes and stir well. Do not allow the garlic to burn. Add the saffron, turmeric, sea salt, and black pepper and mix well until the spices and seasoning evenly coat the shallots and garlic. Pour in the passata and canned tomatoes and stir well, then add the sugar. Reduce the heat to low and cook the sauce for 45 minutes to an hour. You will need to stir the sauce a few times to prevent sticking.

∂ Towards the end of the cooking time, drain and rinse the mussels and clams. Pull the beards off the mussels and give them a gentle scrub.

∂ Once the sauce has reduced and concentrated somewhat, taste it to ensure the seasoning suits your preference. Now begin to add your seafood, starting with the mussels and clams. Give them a good stir to ensure they are well coated with sauce, cover the pan with a lid, and cook for about 5 minutes to allow the shellfish to steam open. Throw in the shrimp and squid, stir well, and cook for 3–4 minutes, then add the scallops. Give the contents of the pan a final stir, then take the pan off the heat and stir in the chopped parsley, reserving just a little. Squeeze over the lemon juice, then serve immediately, garnished with the remaining parsley.

Roasts & grills

Stuffed Eggplants with Lamb, Garlic & Tomatoes
Karniyarik

This Turkish dish is known as *karniyarik*, literally meaning "belly-stuffed," which is exactly what it is—halved eggplants stuffed with ground meat, garlic, and tomatoes. I serve an eggplant half to each of my diners at my Turkish supper clubs and they love it … it's a rather magnificent serving, full of flavors that everyone enjoys. While it is similar to the more famous stuffed-eggplant recipe known as *imam biyaldi*, this version contains meat, which, of course, means that I like it just that little bit more.

SERVES 6

vegetable oil

3 large eggplants, halved lengthways without removing the stalks

2 large onions, roughly diced

1lb 2oz (500g) ground lamb

4 large tomatoes, chopped into 1in (2.5cm) cubes

1 x ¾oz/20g packet of flat leaf parsley, leaves picked and finely chopped

sea salt and freshly ground black pepper

3 long, pale green Turkish peppers or 1 large green bell pepper, cored, deseeded, and cut into ¼in- (4mm-) thick strips

∂ Preheat a large frying pan over medium heat and add a generous amount of vegetable oil. Fry the eggplants, cut-side down, for 8–10 minutes (ensuring they don't blacken), then turn them over and fry them for a further 8 or so minutes. Once cooked, place them on a plate lined with paper towel to absorb some of the excess oil.

∂ Increase the heat a little and fry the onions in the same pan until they begin to brown, then add the lamb and cook, stirring to keep the ingredients moving and prevent the meat from stewing. Once the meat has browned, add 3 of the 4 diced tomatoes, the parsley, and a generous seasoning of sea salt and black pepper, give the mixture a good final stir, then take the pan off the heat.

∂ Preheat the oven to 350°F/180°C. Choose an ovenproof dish that can hold all the eggplant halves.

∂ Using a knife and a spoon, slash the cut side of the fried eggplants without cutting all the way through to the bottom—leave about ½in (1cm) around the edges. Use the spoon to press down and create a cavity in the center of each eggplant half. Divide the stuffing mixture between the eggplant halves. Don't be afraid to pile it high and pat the mixture down with the spoon. Top each one with the remaining diced tomato and the pepper strips and place in the ovenproof dish. Scatter a little cold water over each eggplant to keep it moist in the oven, then bake for 20–25 minutes, or until the pepper is slightly blackened around the edges. Serve immediately.

Saffron & Rosemary Chicken Fillets

This recipe is not especially traditional, as we simply don't use rosemary in the Middle East, but I have added it to my collection of those things-I-found-in-the-pantry moments, which is where my best recipes tend to come from. To hear the words saffron and rosemary in the same sentence doesn't even sound right, but let me reassure you that this combination works and gives the chicken a wonderful flavor along with the punch of garlic.

SERVES 4

2 good pinches of saffron threads

2 tbsp boiling water

1⅓lb (600g) chicken tenders (or use boneless, skinless chicken breasts cut into thick strips)

2 tbsp garlic oil

1½oz (40g) rosemary, leaves picked and very finely chopped

2 heaped tsp crushed sea salt flakes (less if using table salt)

freshly ground black pepper

vegetable oil

∂ Grind the saffron with a mortar and pestle, then pour over the boiling water and leave to infuse for at least 20 minutes until the water has cooled and turned a deep red color.

∂ Place the chicken strips in a bowl and add the garlic oil, finely chopped rosemary, sea salt, a generous seasoning of black pepper, and then the saffron water. Mix well so that the chicken is evenly coated with the marinade, cover the bowl with plastic wrap, and leave in the refrigerator to marinate for 1 hour or so.

∂ Preheat a large frying pan over medium-high heat, drizzle a little oil into the pan, and, without overcrowding the pan, fry the chicken for 3–4 minutes on each side until a nice golden-brown crust forms and they are cooked through. Serve hot alongside a salad such as *Fattoush* (*see* page 183) or Quinoa Salad with Toasted Pistachios, Preserved Lemons & Zucchinis (*see* page 168).

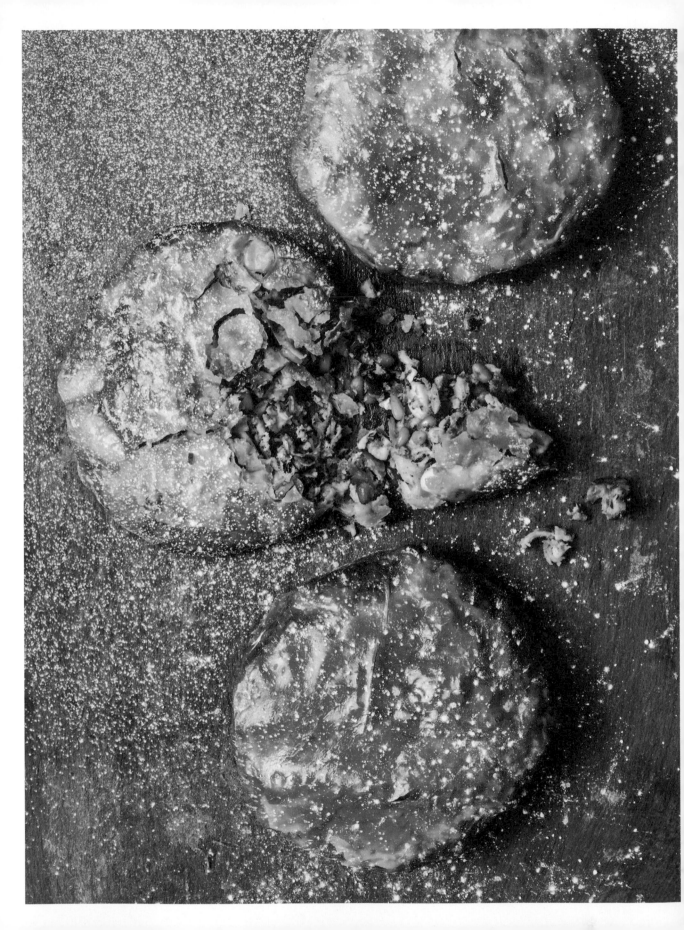

Chicken *Bastilla*

A *bastilla* is the pie equivalent of the Moroccan world and what a pie it is! Aromatic with the spices reminiscent of a souk and filled with chicken (or more traditionally pigeon), it is an opulent dish made for feasting. The meat filling is studded with a classic combination of fruit and nuts (a mixture that draws influence from Persian cuisine), and there are so many flavors and textures in each bite that every mouthful is a real pleasure to savor. This is one of my favorite things to eat—rich and abundant in textures and tastes.

SERVES 6

2¼lb (1kg) onions, diced

olive oil

3in (7.5cm) piece of fresh root ginger, peeled and finely grated

1 heaped tsp ground cinnamon, plus ½ tsp extra to garnish

½ tsp ground mace

½ tsp ground nutmeg

1 tbsp superfine sugar

large handful of dates, pitted and finely chopped

1 medium pre-roasted chicken (about 4½lb /2kg), meat finely shredded

2¾oz (75g) pine nuts, toasted

7 large eggs, 6 hard boiled and roughly chopped, 1 egg separated, the white lightly beaten

1 x ¾oz/20g packet of flat leaf parsley, stalks and leaves finely chopped

1 x ¾oz/20g packet of cilantro, stalks and leaves finely chopped

2 tbsp runny honey

sea salt and freshly ground black pepper

6 sheets (1 packet) of filo pastry, each measuring roughly 19in x 10in (48 x 26cm)

confectioners' sugar, to dust

∂ Preheat the oven to 350°F/180°C. Line a large baking sheet with parchment paper.

∂ Fry the onions in a generous amount of olive oil in a large frying pan set over medium heat, stirring regularly to encourage them to caramelize and prevent burning. Once they are brown (not burned!) and sticky, add the ginger, dry spices, sugar, and dates and stir the mixture well. Cook until any liquid has been absorbed. Remove from the heat and set aside.

∂ Put the shredded chicken into a large bowl with the pine nuts, chopped egg, parsley, and cilantro and mix together. Add the fried onion mixture and honey and give everything another good mix. Season generously with salt and pepper.

∂ Cut each filo pastry sheet in half to make 2 squares. Take 2 squares and overlap them to create a star shape. Divide the mixture into 6 portions, then pile 1 portion into the center of the pastry star. Pat it down to form a flat disc (not too wide, so that you can still seal the pastry edges around the stuffing), then brush the exposed edges of pastry with the beaten egg white. One-by-one, bring the points of the pastry in towards the center and brush each overlap of pastry with a little beaten egg white as you go to secure, until the final flap closes the pastry parcel. Brush with a little more egg white to seal the parcel. Turn the *bastilla* over and place it onto the prepared baking sheet. Repeat with the remaining pastry squares and stuffing to create 6 *bastilla*. Brush the tops and sides of each with egg yolk, then bake for 20–22 minutes, or until golden brown.

∂ Remove the *bastilla* from the oven and, while still hot, dust each with confectioners' sugar and a sprinkling of cinnamon.

Ras el Hanout Chicken Wraps

I came up with this recipe as an alternative to a *shawarma* sandwich; it is less greasy and also such a crowd-pleaser. The key ingredient is the spice blend *ras el hanout*, which in Arabic means "head of the shop"—the name given to the signature blend of the best spices of the shop in which it was made. It is made with a blend of over a dozen spices, often including cumin, cubeb pepper, rose petals, and fenugreek. It is so versatile that it works with meat, poultry, fish, and vegetables. But beware—it packs a punch and it is quite spicy, so don't be too heavy-handed with it. A final dollop of yogurt adds the perfect finishing touch to make every mouthful of this dish utterly satisfying.

SERVES 4–6

2 heaped tbsp *ras el hanout*

olive oil

4 boneless, skinless chicken breasts, chunkier side sliced and spread open for even cooking

sea salt

4–6 flour tortilla wraps

1 red onion, halved and thinly sliced into half moons

pomegranate molasses

arugula leaves and pomegranate seeds to garnish

For the Yogurt Sauce

1 small bunch of mint, leaves picked and finely chopped

2 cups (400g) Greek yogurt

2 tbsp sumac

freshly ground black pepper

∂ Mix the *ras el hanout* with about 4–5 tablespoons of olive oil in a small bowl to create a paste. Smear this over the chicken breasts, ensuring they are well coated. Season each chicken breast with a pinch of sea salt and, if you have time, cover with plastic wrap and leave the chicken in a refrigerator to marinate for as long as needed (but maximum overnight).

∂ To make the yogurt sauce, put the mint into a bowl along with the yogurt, sumac, a generous pinch of sea salt, and some black pepper and mix well until the sumac and mint are evenly incorporated.

∂ Preheat a large frying pan over medium heat if using gas, or medium-high heat if cooking on electric (you may want to use 2 pans at a time if doing all 4 chicken breasts at once), then drizzle in a good amount of olive oil. Put in the chicken breasts and fry them for 8–10 minutes or so on one side and 6–8 minutes on the other side. To check if it is cooked, prod the fattest part of each chicken breast with your finger. If it feels very springy, it needs to cook for a bit longer, but if it feels firm, your chicken is cooked.

∂ Place the chicken on a chopping board and allow it to rest for a few minutes so that the juices can flow back through the meat, ensuring it remains moist and tender. Slice into strips and put several into each wrap with some onion slices. Dollop some of the yogurt on top, drizzle with pomegranate molasses, garnish with arugula and pomegranate seeds, and serve.

Harissa & Preserved Lemon Roasted Poussins

Some of the best recipes in my repertoire were born out of convenience and this dish is one of those. It combines two North African pantry staples, harissa (a popular chili paste) and preserved lemons, to make a delicious marinade that is hard to beat. Poussins (young chickens, around the size of Cornish hens) are common in the Middle East, where they are revered for their tenderness and, even better, are ready in half the time it takes to cook a normal-sized chicken. So this is the perfect recipe for those nights when you come home late and want dinner within the hour. The results are fantastic and a whole poussin per person looks pretty spectacular.

SERVES 4

8 preserved lemons (*see* Tip on page 80)

3 tbsp olive oil

3 tsp crushed sea salt flakes (less if using table salt)

freshly ground black pepper

½ cup (3¼oz/90g) rose harissa paste

4 whole poussins (young chickens)

∂ Using a food processor or hand blender, blitz the preserved lemons, olive oil, salt, pepper to taste, and rose harissa together until you achieve a smooth mixture. Pour this over your poussins and rub the mixture into the birds using your hands.

∂ Preheat the oven to 425°F/220°C. Place the poussins in a large roasting pan or ovenproof dish lined with parchment paper. Roast the poussins for 45–50 minutes until cooked through and nicely browned on top—check the juices run clear when pierced at the thickest part of the thigh. Serve immediately.

∂ **Tip**
You can prepare the poussins in advance and cook them later if you prefer. Just cover the marinated poussins with plastic wrap and leave in the refrigerator up to one day before you are ready to cook.

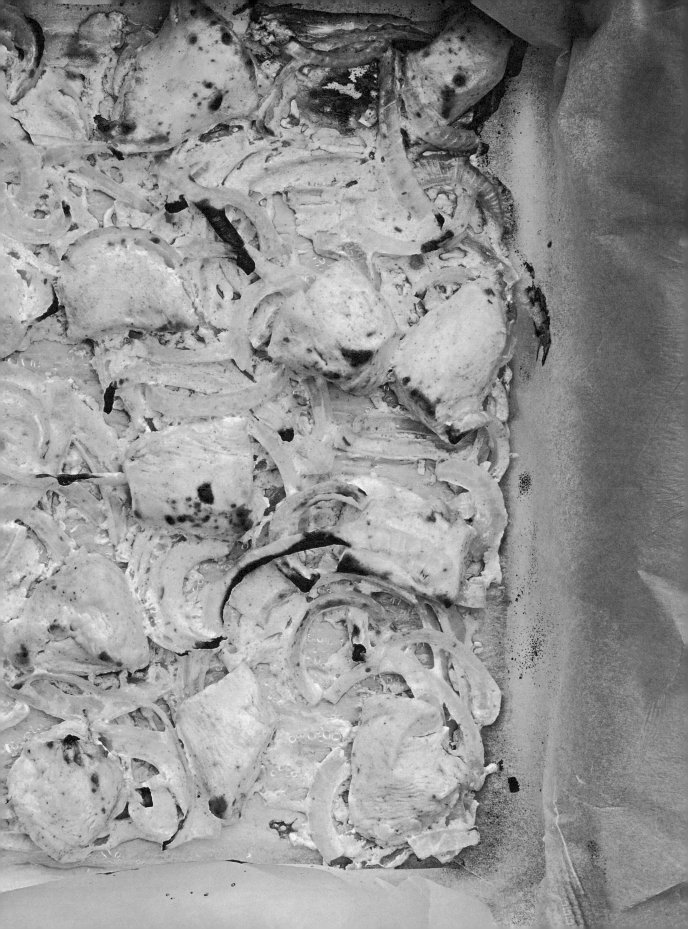

Saffron & Lemon Chicken *Joojeh Kabab*

One of the most popular poultry dishes of Iran, *joojeh kabab* probably features on the menu of every Persian restaurant in the world. Traditionally made using poussin, what really makes this dish so special is the way in which the chicken is marinated in yogurt and lemon juice, which breaks down the fibers and tenderizes the flesh beautifully. The addition of saffron and onions creates the signature flavor that makes this a much-loved dish. This is my simplified version of the recipe, which can be made at home in a conventional oven if, like me, you don't have a barbecue or flame grill.

SERVES 4

4 onions, cut in half and thinly sliced into half moons

juice of 5 lemons

4 tbsp olive oil

1 tsp ground turmeric

2 cups (400g) Greek yogurt

3 tbsp crushed sea salt flakes (less if using table salt)

generous pinch of saffron threads

3 tbsp boiling water

6 large boneless, skinless chicken breasts, cut into 2in (5cm) pieces

∂ Put the onions, lemon juice, olive oil, turmeric, yogurt, and sea salt into a large mixing bowl and mix well. Using a mortar and pestle, grind the saffron to a powder, then pour over the boiling water and leave to infuse for 5–10 minutes.

∂ Add the chicken to the mixing bowl. Mix well to evenly coat the chicken pieces in the yogurt, then add the saffron water to the bowl and mix thoroughly. Cover the bowl with plastic wrap and leave the chicken in the refrigerator to marinate for a minimum of 1 hour or preferably overnight.

∂ Once the chicken has been marinated, preheat the oven or grill to the highest setting possible. Line a large baking sheet with parchment paper.

∂ Remove each piece of chicken from the marinade using a slotted spoon. Lay out all the pieces of chicken on the prepared baking sheet and bake or grill for 18–20 minutes maximum, or until the pieces have slightly charred edges but remain beautifully moist on the insides. Serve with flour tortillas or basmati rice with a little salad and some yogurt.

Lamb & Sour Cherry Meatballs

Iran boasts dozens of versions of meatballs and we Persians love adding fruit to them for a burst of sweetness. I often make these meatballs for guests with a good homemade sauce, which makes the perfect base to plunge them into. You can buy sour cherries frozen or dried, both sweetened and unsweetened. Sweetened sour cherries work best for this recipe, but you can substitute dried cranberries instead.

SERVES 4-6

1lb 2oz (500g) ground lamb

1 onion, ground or very finely chopped

2 large free-range eggs

2 large handfuls of dried sour cherries, pitted and roughly chopped

1 small bunch of cilantro, leaves picked and finely chopped

1 small bunch of dill, leaves picked and finely chopped

2 tsp turmeric

2 tsp ground cumin

2 tsp garlic powder

1 tsp ground cinnamon

4 tsp crushed sea salt flakes (less if using table salt), plus extra to season the sauce

freshly ground black pepper

vegetable oil

For the Tomato Sauce

1½lb (700g) plum tomatoes

1 large garlic bulb, cloves bashed and peeled

1 scant tsp turmeric

1 tsp ground cumin

½ tsp ground cinnamon

2 tsp superfine sugar

1 x 14oz/400g can chopped tomatoes

∂ First prepare the sauce. Preheat a large cooking pot over medium heat if using gas, or medium-high if cooking on electric, and add a good amount of oil to generously coat the base of the pan. Chop each tomato roughly into 3 chunks and add these to the pot along with the garlic cloves, stir well, and allow to cook for about 10 minutes, or until the tomatoes begin to soften. Add the turmeric, cumin, cinnamon, sugar, and a generous amount of salt and black pepper and stir well. Allow the spices to cook out for a further 10 minutes, then add the canned tomatoes and stir well. Cover the pan with a lid, reduce the temperature to very low, and cook the sauce for 1½–2 hours. Stir the sauce every so often to ensure it is not burning. If it reduces too much, add a little bit of boiling water to the pan.

∂ To make the meatballs, preheat a large frying pan over medium heat. Simply put all the ingredients, except the oil, into in a large mixing bowl and, using your hands, mix everything together really well for 6–8 minutes, ensuring you use your fingers to really break up all the clumps of lamb meat so that everything is combined and the mixture is smooth—this will make for light and smooth meatballs.

∂ Preheat a large frying pan over high heat, then drizzle in a little oil. As the pan and oil heat up, roll your meatballs into ping-pong-sized balls and then place them straight into the frying pan. Cook them for roughly 6 minutes on each side. The idea is not to cook them thoroughly but to create a nice brown crust on them to seal the meat. Once browned, place them straight into the tomato sauce and allow them to cook for a further 20–30 minutes before serving. This dish is best served with rice, couscous, or roasted potatoes, or even in wraps.

Mechouia-Style Lamb Leg with Cumin Dipping Salt

While *mechouia* refers to the art of roasting a whole lamb, the *mechouia* style has often been interpreted for Western menus—you slow roast a joint of lamb but use the same traditional cumin dipping salt at the end to season every bite. I like slow cooking a whole leg of lamb, even though I usually prefer my lamb cooked rare, and while slow cooking cooks the meat through fully (which is authentic), it remains tender, juicy, and sweet. Pick up the lamb and dip it in the cumin salt, although, if you prefer to be "civilized," you can use a knife and fork.

SERVES 8

5½lb (2.5kg) leg of lamb on the bone

3½ tbsp (50g) butter, softened

2 tbsp ground coriander

1 tbsp ground cumin

1 tbsp cumin seeds

2 tsp paprika

1 tsp cayenne pepper

1 tsp dried thyme

4 garlic cloves, crushed and peeled

1 tbsp crushed sea salt flakes
(less if using table salt)

freshly ground black pepper

For the Cumin Dipping Salt

2 tbsp cumin seeds

2 tbsp crushed sea salt flakes
(less if using table salt)

pinch of ground cinnamon

∂ Preheat the oven to 300°F/150°C. Line a large roasting pan with parchment paper.

∂ Using a sharp knife, carefully make deep incisions all over the lamb leg so that it can absorb as much of the marinade flavoring as possible.

∂ Put the butter into a small bowl, add the dry spices, thyme, and crushed garlic and blend thoroughly until the mixture forms a paste. Rub this paste all over the lamb leg, pushing it into the incisions you made and working it into the leg as much as possible. Place the lamb leg onto the prepared roasting pan and roast for 5 hours, basting the lamb with its juices every 20–30 minutes or so to ensure it stays moist and hydrated.

∂ Once cooked, remove the lamb from the oven, cover it with foil, and allow the meat to rest for 15 minutes.

∂ Meanwhile, make the cumin dipping salt. Put the cumin seeds in a dry frying pan over medium-high heat and toast, shaking the pan now and then, until they release an aroma, then grind with a mortar and pestle. Combine the ground cumin seeds with the sea salt and cinnamon and place the mixture in a small dish that is suitable for dipping the meat into.

∂ When rested, serve the lamb leg on a platter. The flesh will be moist and succulent and will literally fall off the bone. Serve with Turmeric & Cumin Roasted Potatoes (*see* page 201).

Spiced Rack of Lamb with Pomegranate Sauce

When I was younger, I perceived rack of lamb to be the height of sophistication and considered it best left for eating in fancy restaurants. I never knew just how easy and quick it was to prepare it at home, and now it is something we eat regularly. The pomegranate sauce is a great match for the spicing on the lamb and makes every bite absolutely flavor packed.

SERVES 4

2 tsp cumin seeds

1 tsp coriander seeds

5 tbsp olive oil

1 tsp ground cumin

½ tsp ground cinnamon

½ tsp cayenne pepper

½ tsp ground ginger

½ tsp turmeric

pinch of ground nutmeg

2 racks of lamb, French trimmed

sea salt

For the Pomegranate Sauce

4 tbsp pomegranate molasses

scant ½ cup (100ml) pomegranate juice

1 tbsp runny honey

2 tbsp syrupy balsamic vinegar

∂ Preheat the oven to 400°F/200°C. Put the cumin seeds and coriander seeds in a large, dry heavy-based frying pan over medium-high heat and toast the seeds, shaking the pan now and then, until they release an aroma, then grind with a mortar and pestle.

∂ Combine the olive oil with all the dry spices in a small bowl until they form a paste, then rub the paste all over the racks of lamb, including some on the undersides. Put the pan back on the heat and sear the lamb on all exposed sides until each side becomes lightly browned, which should take no more than a couple of minutes per side.

∂ Transfer the racks of lamb to a roasting dish and season the lamb all over with sea salt. Roast in the oven for about 15 minutes, then remove, cover the dish with foil, and allow the lamb to rest for 6–8 minutes.

∂ While the lamb is resting, make the pomegranate sauce. Pour the cooking juices from the roasting dish into the frying pan in which you seared the lamb, along with the pomegranate molasses, pomegranate juice, honey, and balsamic vinegar and bring the mixture to a gentle boil. Cook until the sauce is glossy and even.

∂ Using a sharp knife, slice through the rack of lamb in between the bones and serve the cutlets immediately, with the pomegranate sauce drizzled over.

Turkish Adana *Köfte* Kebabs

This is one of my favorite Turkish kebabs, hailing from the city of Adana, which is famous for its kebabs. Delicious and spicy, it packs quite a punch, courtesy of the *pul biber* chili flakes, and is utterly addictive. Traditionally, these are long kebabs but, for ease, I tend to make little elongated meatballs (*köfte*) out of the mixture and stuff them into flatbreads with some Greek yogurt or *Cacik* (*see* page 15), sliced onions, a handful of cilantro, and, if you are very brave or are hardened to the heat of chilies, a little extra *pul biber*.

SERVES 4

1lb 2oz (500g) ground lamb
(fat is essential in this recipe,
so do not opt for lean meat)

1 large onion, ground in a food processor
or very finely chopped

3 tsp Aleppo pepper flakes (*pul biber*)

3 garlic cloves, crushed

1 x ¾oz/20g packet of flat leaf parsley,
leaves picked and finely chopped

½ red pepper, cored, deseeded, and very
finely chopped

2 large free-range eggs

2 heaped tsp crushed sea salt flakes
(less if using table salt)

freshly ground black pepper

vegetable oil (if frying)

To serve

flour tortillas or bread of your choice

sliced red onion

chopped parsley

Greek or Turkish or strained yogurt

∂ Put all the ingredients except for the oil into a large mixing bowl and mix them together well. Really work the mixture thoroughly with your hands, pummeling and kneading the meat like bread dough until the texture has broken down and the eggs and herbs are evenly distributed. Take a big fistful of meat and, in the palm of your hand, mold it into a long sausage shape. Flatten the mixture and form a kebab about 6–8in (15–20cm) long and 2in (5cm) wide. Repeat until all the mixture is used up. You can make them longer if you wish, especially if you have the classic long, flat sword-like skewers, around which you can mold the mixture (but small kebabs are just as good). You can also make little patties or meatballs with this mixture.

∂ If you have made mini patties or meatballs, fry them in a preheated frying pan over medium heat for about 7–8 minutes on each side.

∂ If you have opted for a long kebab shape, there are several cooking methods I can suggest. Of course, barbecuing the kebabs over coals is the proper way to do it. Avoid the hottest part of the barbecue and cook them for about 8 minutes on each side until they are nicely charred. Alternatively, cook the kebabs in a little vegetable oil in a frying pan over medium-high heat if using gas, or on full blast on the highest setting if using electric, for approximately 8 minutes on each side until they are nice and brown.

∂ Serve the kebabs in tortilla wraps or bread of your choice, with sliced red onion and chopped parsley. A little yogurt tops the whole thing off very nicely.

Tray-Baked Rose Petal Lamb Chops with Chili & Herbs

What better dish is there than one that can be placed into a roasting pan, thrown in the oven, and is ready in less than 15 minutes? This is the kind of food that I want to eat all the time. It isn't messy or time consuming and the results are truly spectacular. This is a veritable meat feast and, of course, you can use any spices you like, although salt is essential to bring out the flavor, so don't forget to use an adequate amount.

SERVES 4

1¾lb (800g) lamb chops or loin

6 tbsp olive oil

5 tbsp dried edible rose petals, finely ground in a spice grinder

1 heaped tsp turmeric

3 tsp ground cumin

3 tsp cumin seeds

1 tsp ground cinnamon

2 heaped tsp crushed sea salt flakes (less if using table salt)

3 fat garlic cloves, thinly sliced

2 tbsp rosewater

For the Herb & Chili Drizzle

1 large red chili, deseeded and finely chopped

1 x ¾oz/20g packet of cilantro, leaves picked and finely chopped

2 tsp dried mint

juice of ½ lime

8 tbsp olive oil

sea salt and freshly ground black pepper

∂ Put your lamb chops into a large bowl, then add the oil, ground rose petals, spices, sea salt, garlic, and rosewater and mix them into the lamb chops well, ensuring they coat the meat evenly. Cover with plastic wrap and leave the chops in the refrigerator to marinate for a minimum of 1 hour, to allow the flavors to permeate the meat. (You can marinate the lamb chops overnight and cook them the next day.)

∂ Preheat the oven to the highest temperature possible, on a fan assisted setting if you have one. Line a large baking sheet with parchment paper. Lay the lamb chops on the baking sheet with the fat sides up so that they crisp up nicely. Once the oven has been hot for about 20 minutes, put in the lamb and roast for 22 minutes, but check after 20 minutes.

∂ While the lamb is cooking, combine all the ingredients for the drizzle in a small bowl and mix well. Season with sea salt and black pepper according to your preference.

∂ Remove the lamb from the oven and dot generously with the herb and chili drizzle. Serve immediately, with steamed basmati rice.

Lamb & Pistachio Patties
Fistikli Kebap

Based on the Turkish *fistikli kebap*, this is my quick-and-easy version of the classic recipe. I add a few extra ingredients that work well with the pistachios. In the absence of a barbecue or flame grill, I like to shape the mixture into patties, which are easy to cook in a frying pan, but you can shape it into meatballs, larger patties, or elongated kebabs if preferred. Serve this dish with *Cacik* (*see* page 15) or yogurt.

MAKES ABOUT 10

5¼oz (150g) shelled pistachios

2 large free-range eggs

1lb 2oz (500g) ground lamb

1 onion, ground or very finely chopped

2 tsp ground cumin

2 heaped tsp sumac

1 tsp ground coriander

1 tsp dried oregano

zest of 1 lime

3 tbsp crushed sea salt flakes
(less if using table salt)

freshly ground black pepper

1 tbsp vegetable oil

∂ Blitz two-thirds of the pistachios in a food processor until they are finely ground. Lightly pulse the remaining pistachios, then give them just a little rough chop, and put them into a large mixing bowl with the finely ground nuts. Add the remaining ingredients except for the cooking oil to the nuts and mix them together well using your hands. Really work the mixture thoroughly, pummeling and kneading the meat like bread dough until the texture has broken down and the egg and pistachios are evenly distributed.

∂ Preheat a large nonstick frying pan over medium heat and preheat the oven to its lowest setting.

∂ Divide the mixture into 10 balls and shape them into flattened patties. Drizzle enough vegetable oil to coat the base of the preheated frying pan and fry several of the patties at a time, without overcrowding the pan, until the undersides form a nice brown crust, which should take about 6 minutes, then flip them over and cook until both sides are done. Transfer the cooked batch to an ovenproof dish and keep warm in the oven while you fry the remaining patties. Serve with *Cacik* (*see* page 15).

Spice-Perfumed Shoulder of Lamb

Persian spices are aromatic and flavorsome, never harsh or abrasive. Spicing is used in a subtle way and this spice-perfumed lamb is made with my special blend of some of the most commonly used spices, fused with more unique ingredients such as rose petals and lime powder. This particular spice blend works very well with the fatty nature of the shoulder cut of lamb.

SERVES 6

5½lb (2.5kg) shoulder of lamb

2 heaped tbsp sumac

4 tbsp dried edible rose petals

1 tbsp ground cumin

½ tbsp ground cinnamon

½ tbsp dried lime powder (or add 1 extra tbsp sumac)

vegetable oil

2 tsp crushed sea salt flakes (less if using table salt)

∂ Preheat the oven to 320°F/160°C. Place the lamb shoulder in a roasting pan lined with parchment paper.

∂ Put the sumac, rose petals, cumin, cinnamon, and lime powder into a spice grinder or small food processor and process until the rose petals are ground as finely as you can manage.

∂ Drizzle a little oil onto the lamb and rub it all over the joint to create a surface for your spice mixture to stick to, then season generously with the sea salt.

∂ Roast in the oven for 4 hours, then remove the lamb, cover with foil, and leave it to rest for 10 minutes before serving. To serve, you can literally take a fork and gently pull the lamb apart or be all fancy and rather unnecessarily use a knife to slice it. Serve with a green salad, potatoes, or rice.

Seared Beef with Pomegranate & Balsamic Dressing

This is, hands-down, one of the most popular dishes in my entire repertoire. Every time I make it, it only reminds me of one person... my cousin Laily who, whenever we eat together, pleads "Please can you make the pomegranate beef?" This dish of lovely juicy slivers of beef with the sharp yet sweet sauce drizzled over it, finished with brightly colored pomegranate seeds, is a real crowd-pleaser and looks spectacular.

**SERVES 4 AS AN APPETIZER
OR 2 AS A MAIN COURSE**

1lb (400g) flank, sirloin, hanger, or onglet steak (or use lamb neck fillets)

2 tbsp olive oil

sea salt and freshly ground black pepper

1 bag of arugula or watercress or any peppery leaves

3½oz (100g) pomegranate seeds

For the Pomegranate & Balsamic Dressing

generous ¾ cup (200ml) pomegranate molasses

generous ¼ cup (75ml) syrupy balsamic vinegar

1 tbsp olive oil

2 heaped tsp Dijon mustard

∂ Mix the sauce ingredients together in a measuring jug or any vessel with a pouring spout, then set aside.

∂ Preheat a heavy-based frying pan over high heat. Rub the beef with the olive oil and some sea salt and black pepper and place it in the pan (the pan should sizzle and smoke when you put in the beef). Sear the beef for about 3 minutes on each side, then remove it from the pan and allow it to rest so that the juices flow back through the meat, keeping it moist and juicy. To check if the meat is cooked, poke it with your finger. If there is a lot of bounce, the meat is very rare. The less bounce you have, the more the meat is cooked. You are looking for meat that doesn't have too much bounce yet still retains a rare center but, of course, you can cook your meat for longer, if desired (although these particular cuts are not well suited to cooking well-done).

∂ Once the meat has rested for at least 5 minutes, thinly slice the beef into slivers and arrange them on a platter. Take a generous handful of arugula leaves and place in the center of the platter, then drizzle the sauce all over the beef and, finally, garnish with the pomegranate seeds. Serve immediately.

Quince & Pomegranate Glazed Pork

Pork, although not traditionally used in the Middle East, is enjoyed by many and when I think of this meat, I always imagine it in a sticky and sweet sauce. This marinade has fantastic and unusual flavors that work very well with the pork. The fillet is a completely lean cut, but needs every bit of flavor it can get as a result of the lack of fat. Quince is such a special ingredient and, these days, you can find quince paste in most supermarkets near the cheese section. It provides the base for my marinade in this simple but mouthwatering pork dish, which is great served with a simple side salad or even sliced thinly and stuffed into pita bread.

SERVES 4

5¼oz (150g) quince paste (membrillo)

scant ½ cup (100ml) pomegranate juice

1 tbsp pomegranate molasses

2 tbsp honey

2 tsp crushed sea salt flakes
(less if using table salt)

1 tsp ground cumin

½ tsp ground cinnamon

1⅓lb (600g) loin pork fillet

1 tbsp olive oil

∂ Combine the quince paste, pomegranate juice, pomegranate molasses, honey, sea salt, and spices in a small bowl and mix them well (using a fork might help to mash the quince paste down) until the quince paste is thoroughly dissolved.

∂ Roll the pork fillet in the marinade (you can cut it into 2 manageable pieces if preferred), cover the bowl with plastic wrap, and leave in the refrigerator to marinate for a minimum of 1 hour, although the pork will taste much better if marinated overnight.

∂ Preheat the oven to 350°F/180°C. When you are ready to cook the pork, preheat a large ovenproof frying pan over medium heat and add the oil. Shake off any excess marinade (reserve the remaining marinade) and sear the pork fillet for a couple of minutes on each side until it colors and forms a nice seared crust. It may blacken somewhat because of the sugars in the marinade, but don't worry—this doesn't mean the meat is burned. Brush some of the leftover marinade evenly onto the pork fillet and transfer the pan to the oven for a further 10 minutes, then remove from the oven and allow it to rest for 5 minutes.

∂ While the pork rests, pour the remaining marinade into a small pan and heat gently until it bubbles. Once rested, cut the fillet into 2in- (5cm-) thick medallions or thinly slice. Serve with a drizzle of the marinade.

Cod in Tamarind, Cilantro & Fenugreek Sauce
Ghelyeh Mahi

Based on the Persian dish known as *ghelyeh mahi* from the Bandar port region (which is essentially a seafood stew) my version uses cod, but you can use any fish you like as a substitute. The tamarind adds a sour note to the sauce, which is a popular characteristic of many *Bandari* dishes and doesn't overpower the fish at all. The addition of a little heat from cayenne pepper makes this dish feel almost more Indian than Persian, but a lot of the spicing in this region of Iran draws influence from the bold flavors of the neighboring states of the Persian Gulf. This dish is traditionally served with rice.

SERVES 4-6

vegetable oil

1 large onion, finely chopped

1 tbsp all-purpose flour

6 garlic cloves, bashed and thinly sliced

1 tsp turmeric

2 tsp dried fenugreek leaves

½ tsp cayenne pepper

pinch of superfine sugar

1 large bunch of cilantro,
stalks and leaves finely chopped

1 tbsp tamarind paste

generous 2 cups (500ml) warm water

1⅓lb (600g) cod loin
(or use any firm-fleshed white fish)

sea salt and freshly ground black pepper

∂ Set a large frying pan over medium heat and pour in enough oil to coat the base of the pan. Fry the onion until it becomes translucent and just begins to turn golden at the edges. Add the flour and stir it into the onion well to cook it out, then drizzle a little more oil into the pan and add the garlic slivers, too (ensure you don't let them brown or burn). Add the turmeric, fenugreek, cayenne, and sugar and stir well for 1–2 minutes.

∂ Stir the cilantro into the onion-and-garlic mixture and cook until it begins to soften. Dissolve the tamarind paste into the warm water, then pour it into the pan, reduce the heat to a moderate setting, cover the pan (leaving a little gap open), and simmer for about 15 minutes.

∂ Once the cooking time has elapsed, cut each cod loin into 2in (5cm) pieces and lay them on top of the sauce, spooning just enough of the sauce over them to barely cover each piece of fish. Season to taste with a little sea salt and black pepper, then cover the pan with a lid and cook for a further 15 minutes with the lid on. Serve immediately.

Shrimp with Sumac, Cilantro, Lemon & Garlic

Sumac has very citric properties. Traditionally, we use it to season grilled lamb kebabs, although it is now sprinkled onto everything and used in many different ways. It works especially well with seafood and white meats, as the citrusy flavor really complements them. I love using it with shrimp; it adds flecks of color to them and gives a lovely flavor to the finished dish. I like to buy the biggest shrimp I can find (and keep just the heads and tails on), but you can use whichever kind you like best.

SERVES 4

6 tbsp olive oil

zest of 2 lemons and juice of ½ lemon

2 tbsp sumac

5 large garlic cloves, bashed, peeled, and thinly sliced

1 x ¾oz/20g packet of cilantro, stalks and leaves finely chopped

sea salt and freshly ground black pepper

1¾lb (800g) peeled raw jumbo shrimp

∂ Select a wide, shallow vessel in which to make your marinade. Put in the olive oil, then add the lemon zest, sumac, garlic, and cilantro. Season well with a generous amount of sea salt and black pepper, add the lemon juice, and mix the ingredients together well.

∂ Place the shrimp in the marinade and mix well to ensure they are evenly coated, then cover the dish with plastic wrap and marinate for at least 30 minutes in the refrigerator if you can. Of course, you can cook the shrimp immediately, but a little marinating time will allow the flavors to permeate them. As the marinade contains acid (lemon juice), I would not recommend marinating the shrimp for longer than a few hours, since it may partially cook them (although they will still be perfectly safe to eat).

∂ Preheat a large frying pan over medium-high heat. Once it is hot, shake off the excess marinade from each shrimp and place it straight into the frying pan. Cook the shrimp for 2–3 minutes on each side until they turn pink, and serve immediately.

Citrus-Spiced Salmon

Salmon is a great fish to spice up. Its oily nature and robust flavor allow it to hold spicing and gutsy marinades well without being overpowered, and the spice mixture for this dish is really quite bold. We all know that citrus goes well with fish and as well as squeezing over lemon juice, I use orange and lime zest to produce a citrusy zing. The whole thing takes no more than 15 minutes to prepare, cook, and serve. What on earth could be better than that?

SERVES 6

4 tbsp dried edible rose petals, finely ground

2 tsp sumac

1 tsp dried lime powder

1 tsp ground cumin

½ tsp ground cinnamon

zest of 1 orange

zest of 1 lime

3–6 tbsp olive oil

6 skinless salmon fillets, about ¼lb (100g) each

sea salt and freshly ground black pepper

lemon wedges, to serve

∂ Preheat the oven to 400°F/200°C (preferably fan assisted for this recipe, as a higher heat gives better results). Line a baking sheet with parchment paper.

∂ Combine the ground rose petals, spices, and grated orange and lime zest in a small bowl, add the olive oil and stir well to form a wet marinade for the salmon.

∂ Rub each salmon fillet well with the spice marinade and place it on the prepared baking sheet. (At this stage you can cover with plastic wrap and leave overnight in the refrigerator to marinate, if you wish.) Once all the fillets are well coated in the marinade, season them well with sea salt and black pepper, then bake for 10–12 minutes until the fish is cooked through. I like to serve this with lemon wedges and a *Fattoush* Salad (*see* page 183).

Belly-Stuffed Rainbow Trout
Mahi Shekampor

Literally meaning "belly-stuffed fish," **Mahi shekampor is a classic recipe from southern Iran.** I like to use rainbow trout for this recipe, but you can use any whole fish you like. My addition of preserved lemons give the stuffing a wonderful citrusy kick that provides the perfect accompaniment to the trout, so there's no need for additional lemon to season your fish.

SERVES 4

2¾oz (75g) pine nuts

olive oil

1 garlic bulb, cloves bashed, peeled and thinly sliced

2 red chilies, thinly sliced

1 bunch of scallions, thinly sliced

1 large bunch of cilantro, stalks and leaves roughly chopped

4 preserved lemons, finely chopped

2 large whole rainbow trout, roughly 1⅓lb (600g) each, gutted and scaled

sea salt and freshly ground black pepper

∂ Preheat the oven to 400°F/200°C. Line a baking sheet with parchment paper. Scatter the pine nuts on the baking sheet and toast them in the oven for 3–4 minutes, checking them frequently to prevent burning. Once toasted, set aside.

∂ Set a large frying pan over medium heat, drizzle in enough olive oil to coat the base of the pan generously, then add the garlic and chilies and stir well to prevent burning. Once the garlic is translucent, add the scallion slices, followed by the cilantro stalks and leaves, give everything a good stir, and cook until the herbs and scallions soften. Add the preserved lemons, stir well again, then add the toasted pine nuts. Give the ingredients a last stir, then take the pan off the heat and allow the contents to cool for at least 15 minutes.

∂ Place the whole trout onto the same paper-lined baking sheet you used to toast the pine nuts. Open up the belly cavities of the fish, divide the stuffing mixture into 2, and pack 1 portion of the stuffing into the belly and head cavities of each fish. Once done, drizzle a little olive oil on to the fish skins, season well with sea salt and black pepper, and bake for 25–30 minutes (or less, if your fish are smaller). Once cooked, serve immediately. Two people can share each fish.

Scallops & Shaved Fennel with Saffron, Honey & Citrus Vinaigrette

Scallops are my favorite shellfish—delicate, sweet morsels of flesh that are so versatile you can eat them raw, seared, poached, or baked. This is such an elegant dish, with a little crunch of shaved fennel and a sweet and aromatic dressing, pungent with saffron and citrus notes. Choose the fattest scallops you can find.

SERVES 4

2 large fennel bulbs, ends trimmed

juice of ½ lemon

olive oil

sea salt and freshly ground black pepper

12 large scallops

For the dressing

2 tbsp runny honey

pinch of saffron threads, crumbled

1 tbsp white wine vinegar

juice of 1 orange

little squeeze of lime juice

2 tbsp olive oil

∂ First make the dressing. In a small saucepan, dissolve the honey and crumbled saffron threads in the vinegar and orange and lime juices over low-medium heat. Warm the mixture gently, allowing the saffron to infuse the liquid, but do not let it bubble or boil. Once the mixture begins to take on a golden color from the saffron, give it a stir, and season with a little sea salt. Turn off the heat and set aside.

∂ Shave or thinly slice the fennel and place in a mixing bowl. Mix the lemon juice and 2 teaspoons of olive oil together, season with sea salt and black pepper, then toss over the fennel to prevent it from turning brown and set aside.

∂ Preheat a large frying pan over medium-high heat. Drizzle a little olive oil into the pan and pan-fry the scallops on each side for about 1 minute (or less, if you are using smaller scallops). Remove the scallops from the heat and arrange them on a serving platter with the shaved fennel.

∂ Add the olive oil to the dressing and whisk well until it is amalgamated, then drizzle the dressing over the scallops and fennel and serve immediately.

Za'atar Cod with Relish

If I were allowed to take only three spice blends with me to a dessert island, za'atar would have to be one of them. It is so delicate yet so versatile and can be applied to everything from meat and fish to grains and breads alike. I like to make a quick paste of it with some oil and rub it onto fish before frying. What really makes this dish is the vibrant, citrus-spiked fresh relish that goes with it.

SERVES 4 AS AN APPETIZER OR LIGHT MEAL, OR 2 AS A MAIN MEAL

....

2 heaped tbsp za'atar

olive oil

1lb (400g) prime cod fillet or loin, cut into either 2 or 4 pieces, or other firm white fish

sea salt

For the relish

24 Kalamata olives

6 preserved lemons

8 pickled chilies

1 small bunch of cilantro

olive oil

∂ Mix the za'atar with 4 tablespoons olive oil in a small bowl to create a paste. Smear this paste over the cod pieces, ensuring they are well coated. Season each piece of fish with just a pinch of sea salt and, if you have time, cover with plastic wrap and leave in the refrigerator to marinate until you are ready to cook (but maximum overnight).

∂ To make the relish, remove the pits from the olives and roughly chop the pitted olives. Put them in a bowl. Halve your preserved lemons, remove and discard any seeds, then roughly chop them and add them to the bowl. Thinly slice the pickled chilies, then give them a rough chop, too, before adding them to the bowl. Lastly, roughly chop the cilantro stalks and leaves (the stalks have much flavor) and add to the bowl with a generous glug of olive oil. Mix the ingredients well and set the relish aside. Do not season it with salt as the mixture will be salty enough already from the various ingredients.

∂ Preheat a large frying pan over medium heat, then drizzle in a generous amount of olive oil. Fry your cod fillets for about 8 minutes on one side and just 3–4 minutes on the other. Once golden brown, with a nice spice crusting, serve with a generous helping of the relish and either rice or potatoes on the side.

Bandari Monkfish Tails

The term *Bandari* signifies anything that comes from a port, but is usually a reference to the southern port of Bandar Abbas in Iran. When applied to food, *Bandari* indicates the use of spice in a dish. This simple fish dish is rubbed using a special spice mix made with fresh herbs and aromatics that permeates the fish with a wonderful heady flavor. *Shirazi* Salad (*see* page 178) is the perfect accompaniment to this dish.

SERVES 4

½ tsp turmeric

½ tsp curry powder

½ tsp ground cumin

½ tsp ground coriander

¼ tsp ground cinnamon

2 fat garlic cloves, minced

2 in (5cm) piece of fresh root ginger, peeled and minced

handful of cilantro, leaves picked and finely chopped, plus extra to serve

handful of dill, leaves picked and finely chopped

finely grated zest and juice of 1 lime

2 tbsp Greek yogurt

olive oil

1 tsp crushed sea salt flakes (less if using table salt)

¼ tsp freshly ground black pepper

4 monkfish tails or loins, about 6–7oz (175–200g) each, skinned and cleaned

∂ Mix all the dry spices together in a bowl and add the garlic, ginger, fresh herbs, lime zest and juice, yogurt, and a couple of tablespoons of olive oil. Season with the sea salt and black pepper. Stir well using a fork to break up any clumps of spices. Cover the bowl with plastic wrap and set aside for at least 30 minutes to allow the spice paste to rest.

∂ Place the monkfish tails in a shallow dish. Give the spice paste a good stir and pour it over the fish. Use your hands to really work the paste into the fish, ensuring all sides get an even coating of the mixture. Cover the dish with plastic wrap and place it in the refrigerator for a maximum of 1 hour. Once marinated, remove from the refrigerator and bring the fish to room temperature.

∂ Preheat a frying pan over medium-high heat. When the pan is nice and hot, drizzle a little olive oil into the pan. Gently lay the monkfish in the pan and cook for approximately 5 minutes on each side, or until opaque and firm. Transfer the monkfish tails from the pan to serving plates, leave to rest for 1–2 minutes, then serve with a little extra cilantro sprinkled on top.

Salads & vegetables

Blood Orange & Radicchio Salad

Wonderfully visual, this salad is the perfect accompaniment to Middle Eastern meals because the orange provides a much-needed palate-cleansing acidity. This is one of my favorite side dishes and is simple yet vibrant. Blood oranges are in season in the winter, but you can easily substitute normal oranges for a similarly vibrant result.

SERVES 4–6 AS A SIDE DISH

2 heads of radicchio Trevisano

5 blood oranges

2 tsp sumac

generous handful of dill, leaves picked and finely chopped

For the vinaigrette

4 tbsp olive oil

2 tbsp pomegranate molasses

1 tbsp red wine vinegar

sea salt

freshly ground black pepper

∂ Wash each radicchio head and trim off the base stalk. Cut each radicchio widthways into 1½in- (4cm-) thick slices, fan out the pieces, and place them in a salad bowl.

∂ To peel the blood oranges, cut off a small disc of outer peel from the top and bottom of the fruit and, using a sharp knife, cut away the outer skin past the white pith until you reach exposed flesh. Repeat until all the pith and peel is removed. Cut the oranges in half (cut from top to bottom), then cut each half into ¼in- (8mm-) thick half-moon slices. Add all the slices to the salad bowl along with the sumac and chopped dill.

∂ To make the dressing, place the oil, pomegranate molasses, and vinegar in a bowl with a generous seasoning of sea salt and black pepper and whisk the mixture well until it is evenly combined. Pour the dressing over the salad and, using your hands, toss the ingredients generously through the dressing until everything is evenly coated and the sumac and dill are well distributed. Shake off the excess dressing to serve.

Barley Salad with Griddled Broccolini & Za'atar

Za'atar is one of my favorite spice blends, although it is actually a mixture of wild thyme, salt, and sesame seeds (and sometimes marjoram, oregano, sumac, or cumin), so perhaps "herb blend" would be more accurate. It provides a lovely aromatic flavor to many dishes and offers a fantastic way of livening up a humble grain such as barley; adding a few vegetables makes a real meal of it. Not only is this dish healthy and a colorful treat for the eyes but it bursts with flavor, too.

SERVES 5-6 AS A SIDE DISH

10oz (300g) cherry tomatoes, halved

5 small or 3 large red onions, roughly chopped

sea salt and freshly ground black pepper

10oz (300g) broccolini

½lb (250g) pearl barley

juice of 2 lemons

3 heaped tbsp za'atar

1 small bunch of flat leaf parsley, leaves picked and finely chopped

2 long red chilies (the large, not-so-hot ones), deseeded and finely chopped

2¾oz (75g) pea shoots

3–4 tbsp olive oil

1 cup (250ml) Greek yogurt

3 tsp ground coriander

∂ Preheat the oven to 320°F/160°C. Line a large baking sheet with parchment paper. Place the tomatoes cut-side up on the prepared baking sheet and roast for about 1½ hours, or until partially dehydrated but not burned. Remove from the oven and allow to cool.

∂ Increase the oven temperature to 400°F/200°C. Place the chopped onions in a baking dish, season with salt and pepper, and roast for about 35–45 minutes, or until browned and slightly charred around the edges. Set aside and allow to cool.

∂ Preheat a griddle pan or a heavy-based saucepan over high heat until very hot. Put in the broccolini and season with salt and pepper. Blacken the broccolini stems in the pan—you don't need to cook them through, you just want them to take on a charred flavor; this should take 3 minutes or so on each side. Set aside to cool.

∂ Boil the barley as per the package instructions, then rinse well in cold water, drain, and transfer to a very large mixing bowl. Dress it with half the lemon juice, salt, pepper, and the za'atar. Add the roasted cherry tomatoes and red onions and mix well.

∂ Chop each broccolini stem into 2–3 pieces, incorporate into the salad, and taste to see if more seasoning is needed. Add the chopped parsley, chili, and pea shoots and mix again.

∂ To make the yogurt dressing, add the olive oil to the yogurt along with the remaining lemon juice, the ground coriander, and a generous seasoning of salt and pepper.

∂ Place the salad on a large flat plate, arranging the vegetables nicely around the plate. Finally, drizzle the yogurt sauce all over the salad and serve.

Radish, Cucumber & Red Onion Salad with Mint & Orange Blossom Dressing

Middle Eastern food can be heavy and plentiful so, to balance it out, you need to pair it with light, refreshing dishes that cleanse the palate and aid digestion. This is just that kind of dish—it is a perfect accompaniment to meat and poultry dishes, providing a lovely fresh flavor—and it looks beautiful, too. The lightly sweetened dressing counteracts the acidity, and I just love the intense crunchiness.

SERVES 6 AS A SIDE DISH

½lb (200g) radishes, trimmed and very thinly sliced

1 cucumber

2 small red onions, cut in half and thinly sliced into half moons

2½oz (70g) pine nuts, toasted

For the Mint & Orange Blossom Dressing

1 tbsp runny honey

1½ tsp orange blossom water

juice of 1 lemon

4 tbsp olive oil

sea salt

freshly ground black pepper

2 x ¾oz/20g packets of mint, leaves picked and coarsely chopped

∂ Place the very thinly sliced radishes in a large bowl. Personally, I like both the skin and the seeds of the cucumber, but if you prefer, you can peel the skin, then halve the cucumber lengthways and scoop out and discard the seeds. Slice each cucumber half thinly into half moons and add these to the bowl along with the red onions. Give everything a good mix.

∂ Make your dressing in a separate bowl. Put in the honey, orange blossom water, and lemon juice and stir until the honey has dissolved, then add the olive oil, sea salt, black pepper, and, lastly, the chopped mint. Pour the dressing over the salad, coating all the ingredients well, then add the toasted pine nuts. Toss the salad one last time and serve immediately.

French Lentil & Quinoa Salad with Lemon & Sumac

Quinoa is my pantry staple and I embrace it for all its perceived health benefits and nutritional value. But let's be honest—flavor-wise it doesn't have a lot going for it. However, if you combine it with some herbs, a little citrus, and some lovely French (Puy) lentils, it is transformed from bland to brilliant. This salad is a meal in itself, although a little grilled chicken or grilled haloumi on the side makes a brilliant accompaniment.

SERVES 6-8 AS A SIDE DISH

7oz (200g) quinoa

9oz (250g) French lentils

1lb 2oz (500g) baby tomatoes (I use Pomodorinos or baby plum), halved

3½oz (100g) flat leaf parsley, stalks and leaves finely chopped

2 x ¾oz/20g packets of mint, leaves picked and finely chopped

1 x ¾oz/20g packet of cilantro, stalks and leaves finely chopped

1 bunch of scallions, thinly sliced

3-4 tbsp olive oil

juice of 2-3 lemons

1 heaped tbsp sumac

sea salt

freshly ground black pepper

∂ Cook the quinoa and lentils separately as per their package instructions. Rinse well in cold water, drain, and set aside.

∂ Put the tomatoes, chopped herbs, scallions, olive oil, and lemon juice into a large mixing bowl along with the sumac. Add several generous pinches of crushed sea salt and a generous amount of black pepper and mix the ingredients well. Add the quinoa and lentils and mix well to ensure the ingredients are evenly mixed through the salad and that the dressing coats the quinoa and lentils throughout. Taste the salad and adjust the seasoning if required.

∂ I like to refrigerate this salad for 1-2 hours before serving to allow the flavors to work their way into the quinoa and lentils. Serve with grilled fish, chicken, or haloumi, or, if you are feeling lazy, just crumble in some feta cheese to make a meal of it.

Pomegranate *Tabbouleh* Cups

Tabbouleh is a Levantine salad that has become a staple in so many cultures, and each variation seems to be a slightly tweaked version of the original dish. My version mirrors the authentic recipe, except for the addition of pomegranate seeds. I grew up eating *tabbouleh*, since it's one of the only dishes my mom would make regularly. She taught me how to eat it—by using lettuce leaves to scoop up the salad. The addition of juicy pomegranate seeds gives it a sweet burst. I like to dish it up in Gem lettuce leaves and serve the "cups" to guests. They look beautiful and taste wonderful, too.

MAKES 15 CUPS AS FINGER FOOD OR SERVES 5–6 AS A SIDE DISH

2 heaped tbsp (1oz/25g) bulgar

1 large bunch of flat leaf parsley, leaves picked and finely chopped

3 plum tomatoes, deseeded and finely diced

4 scallions, thinly sliced right up to 3in (7cm) from the ends

½ tsp ground cinnamon

3½oz (100g) pomegranate seeds

1–2 tbsp olive oil

juice of 1 lemon

sea salt and freshly ground black pepper

15 little gem lettuce leaves

∂ Cook the bulgar as per the package instructions, then rinse well in cold water, drain, and transfer to a large bowl.

∂ Mix all your chopped ingredients into the bulgar, along with the cinnamon and pomegranate seeds. Drizzle with the olive oil—add just enough to ensure the mixture is well coated, but not enough to make it greasy. Now add the lemon juice, and sea salt and black pepper to taste.

∂ Take a generous tablespoon of the *tabbouleh* and place it in the depression of a lettuce leaf. Put the "cup" on a serving platter and repeat until all the *tabbouleh* has been used up. Serve the cups on the platter as a salad, or on plates alongside a main dish.

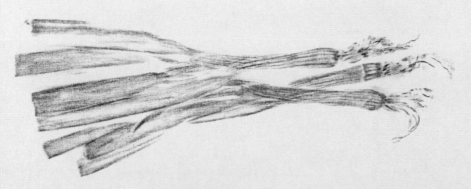

Tomato Salad with Pomegranate Molasses
Gavurdagi Salatasi

The first time I had this salad in Istanbul, I was staggered by its marvelous simplicity. How could a little drizzle of pomegranate molasses transform a simple tomato salad into something so bold and delicious? This salad is really special and makes the perfect accompaniment to any meal. Each time I make it someone asks for the recipe, thinking that the dressing is something special I have conjured up, but nobody ever guesses that the magic ingredient is simply a good drizzle of pomegranate molasses. For this dish, I like to use baby plum tomatoes or, in summer, lovely yellow and green tomato varieties.

SERVES 6 AS A SIDE DISH

1lb 5oz (600g) tomatoes

2 long green Turkish peppers, cut into thin rings, or 1 green bell pepper, thinly sliced lengthways

1 large red onion, cut in half and thinly sliced into half moons

2 tsp sumac, plus a little extra to garnish

4 tbsp pomegranate molasses

sea salt

extra virgin olive oil

3½oz (100g) walnut pieces, to garnish

∂ If using large tomatoes, chop them into rough ¾in (2cm) cubes, or, if using cherry or baby plum tomatoes, simply halve them. There is no science or precision to making this salad—you just chop the tomatoes as you like.

∂ Arrange the tomatoes, pepper rings or strips, and onion on a flat serving plate.

∂ In another bowl combine the sumac, pomegranate molasses, crushed sea salt to taste, and a little drizzle of extra virgin olive oil and give the ingredients a good mix. Drizzle the dressing evenly over the salad. Garnish with the walnuts and a little sprinkling of sumac and serve.

Turkish White Bean Salad
Piyaz

Piyaz is a staple salad of Turkey. This is the Anatolyan version, which uses tahini to give the salad an added dimension. I can quite happily eat this as a meal in itself without any accompaniment. The dressing provides just the right amount of acidity to cut through the richness of the tahini, and lots of onions add great bite and flavor.

SERVES 4–5 AS A SIDE DISH

2 x 14oz/400g cans cannellini beans, drained and rinsed

2 red onions, cut in half and thinly sliced into half moons

1–2 tbsp Aleppo pepper flakes (*pul biber*)

2 x ¾oz/20g packets of flat leaf parsley, leaves picked and roughly chopped

1 fat garlic clove, crushed

juice of 1½ lemons

3 tbsp tahini

3 tbsp olive oil

2 tbsp red wine vinegar

sea salt

freshly ground black pepper

∂ Put the cannellini beans, red onion slices, Aleppo pepper flakes, and chopped flat leaf parsley into a large salad bowl and mix well.

∂ To make your dressing, put the garlic into a separate bowl, then add the lemon juice and tahini and mix well until smooth. Lastly, incorporate the olive oil, red wine vinegar, and a generous amount of crushed sea salt and black pepper and mix the dressing until smooth. If you need a little more liquid, add some cold water until you achieve a consistency that is sufficiently thin enough to dress the salad.

∂ Pour the dressing over the salad, mix everything carefully so as not to smash or break up the beans, then taste the ingredients and adjust the seasoning, if desired, before serving.

Bulgar Salad
Kisir

What the Turks can do with simple bulgar is always pretty impressive to me. This dish makes a great cold accompaniment to a meal and is usually served as part of a big Turkish feast, but I like to serve it with grilled chicken to make a meal, or spooned into some flatbread or a tortilla with a little feta cheese for a great sandwich. You can also serve it with little gem lettuce and use the leaves to scoop it up. *Kisir* can be spicy or not, but this version packs plenty of punch, so omit the chili if you prefer.

SERVES 4 AS A SIDE DISH

½lb (250g) bulgar

⅔ cup (160ml) boiling water

1 tbsp hot pepper paste

juice of 1 lemon

2 tbsp tomato paste

2 tbsp pomegranate molasses

5 tbsp extra virgin olive oil

2 tsp crushed sea salt flakes
(less if using table salt)

freshly ground black pepper

5 ripe tomatoes, finely diced

1 bunch of scallions, finely chopped

1 x ¾oz/20g packet of mint,
leaves picked and finely chopped

1 x ¾oz/20g packet of flat leaf parsley,
leaves picked and finely chopped

3½oz (100g) pomegranate seeds

∂ Tip the bulgar into a shallow dish and pour the hot water over it. Once absorbed (this takes about 15 minutes), transfer to a large bowl.

∂ Add the hot pepper paste, lemon juice, tomato paste, pomegranate molasses, extra virgin olive oil, sea salt, and black pepper to the bulgar and work them into the grains using your hands. Now stir in the tomatoes, scallions, fresh herbs, and the pomegranate seeds until everything is combined. Taste the dish and adjust the seasoning or add more lemon juice, if required.

∂ Allow the dish to rest for about 10 minutes before serving.

Quinoa Salad with Toasted Pistachios, Preserved Lemons & Zucchinis

Quinoa needs a little help in the flavor department, but it doesn't take a lot of imagination to transform this ancient grain into something more special altogether. Being Persian, I have a thing for pistachios (as you will see from the number of recipes in which they appear throughout this book)—toast them in a pan, almost burning them, and they take on a smoky depth that makes a great addition to this dish. Preserved lemons are naturally salty and provide much-needed seasoning for quinoa, too.

SERVES 4–6 AS A SIDE DISH

5¼oz (150g) quinoa, rinsed

3½oz (100g) shelled pistachios

olive oil

2 large zucchinis, cut into ½in- (1cm-) thick slices

1 small bunch of mint, leaves picked and finely chopped

6–8 preserved lemons, deseeded and finely chopped

juice of ½ lemon

sea salt

freshly ground black pepper

2 heaped tsp nigella seeds

∂ Put the quinoa in a saucepan, cover with water, and bring to a boil. Reduce the heat and simmer for 15 minutes, then strain and rinse in cold running water until the grains are cold. Allow the excess moisture to drain, then put the quinoa into a large mixing bowl.

∂ In a large frying pan set over medium heat, toast the pistachios without any oil for just 3–4 minutes, gently tossing them to ensure they do not blacken too much or burn, then set aside.

∂ Drizzle just the tiniest amount of oil into the same frying pan and fry the zucchinis for 3 minutes on each side until they get a good color on them but are not cooked all the way through. Transfer the slices to a chopping board and chop each slice in half.

∂ Add the zucchini to the quinoa along with the chopped mint, preserved lemons, 3 tablespoons of olive oil, the lemon juice, and sea salt and black pepper to taste and mix well. Lastly, add the toasted pistachios and the nigella seeds and give the ingredients one final mix. Serve immediately.

Salad *Olivieh*

One of the most popular salads in Iran, Salad *Olivieh* is believed to have taken its influence from Russia and the *salade Russe*, made with potatoes, peas, carrots, and mayonnaise. Naturally, we have made it our own—we have removed the carrot and added chicken, boiled eggs, and cucumber, which improve it greatly in my opinion. I also like to add scallions and cilantro, and lighten it with a combination of Greek yogurt and mayonnaise so that it doesn't feel as rich and heavy. It is often eaten as a sandwich filling, which is strangely good, too. (Don't knock it, 'til you've tried it...)

SERVES 8-10

1lb 10oz (750g) waxy potatoes (Yukon Gold or fingerling potatoes work well)

1 medium whole roast chicken, skin and bones removed, meat finely shredded

10½oz (300g) pickles or cornichons (preferably in brine, not vinegar), finely diced

2 bunches of scallions, thinly sliced

8 large free-range eggs, hard boiled and roughly chopped

1 large bunch of cilantro, leaves picked and finely chopped

5¼oz (150g) fresh or frozen peas, boiled for just a couple of minutes, then drained

4 tbsp mayonnaise

juice of 1 lemon, plus extra to taste

6 tbsp Greek yogurt

2 tbsp olive oil

sea salt

freshly ground black pepper

∂ Bring a large saucepan of water to a boil and boil the potatoes until they are cooked through. Be careful not to overcook them—around 12 minutes usually does the trick, depending on their size. Drain, then immediately plunge them into iced water to stop them overcooking. Once cooled, drain and roughly chop them into 1in (2.5cm) chunks.
∂ In the largest mixing bowl you can find, combine the potatoes with the shredded chicken, diced pickles, scallions, egg, cilantro, and peas. Using your hands, lightly toss them together, trying to avoid crushing them as much as possible.
∂ In a small bowl, mix the mayonnaise, lemon juice, Greek yogurt, and olive oil together with a generous amount of salt and black pepper. Pour the dressing over the salad ingredients and mix well using a wooden spoon. Some of the potato and egg will eventually get crushed and work its way into the salad dressing, which is exactly what should happen, so don't worry—it makes the dish really tasty. Check the seasoning is to your liking and adjust the salt, pepper, or lemon juice, if desired. Refrigerate the salad for at least 1 hour before serving.

Chicken & Artichoke Salad with Yogurt Dressing

I do like a good grilled chicken salad, but to be honest, I'm slightly over chicken Caesar salad, as the dressing alone racks up hundreds of calories and it's not quite the light lunch I once believed it to be. I started using yogurt dressings for salads years ago and think they are highly underrated. For the salad itself, I prefer leaves such as watercress and arugula, as these have bold flavors that add punch to the dish instead of wilting in among the other ingredients. And I adore preserved artichoke hearts! I can eat them with and in everything, so it's clear why this salad has become one of my favorites.

SERVES 4–6

6 boneless, skinless chicken breasts

olive oil, for brushing

sea salt

freshly ground black pepper

10½oz (300g) watercress

1lb 2oz (500g) artichoke hearts preserved in oil, drained and halved

3½oz (100g) walnut pieces

1 x ¾oz/20g packet of chives, each stem snipped into 3

1 x ¾oz/20g packet of flat leaf parsley, leaves picked and barely chopped

1 x ¾oz/20g packet of mint, leaves picked and barely chopped

2 red onions, cut in half and thinly sliced into half moons

2 long red chilies, thinly sliced into rings

10½oz (300g) feta cheese

For the Yogurt Dressing

1½ cups (300g) Greek yogurt

1 fat garlic clove, crushed

1 tbsp sumac

1 tsp dried mint

zest of 2 lemons and juice of 1½ lemons

4 tbsp olive oil

∂ Preheat a griddle pan (or a frying pan, if you prefer) over high heat. Place the chicken breasts between two layers of plastic wrap and and flatten them out to an even thickness by pounding them with a rolling pin or meat mallet. Start pounding from the center of each breast and work outwards towards the edges. Brush each flattened chicken breast with olive oil and season on both sides with sea salt and black pepper. Griddle the chicken breast for approximately 6 minutes (depending on the thickness of the breasts) on each side until they are cooked through. Remove the chicken breasts from the heat and allow to rest.

∂ To make the dressing, combine the dressing ingredients in a small bowl with sea salt and black pepper to taste and stir well until they are evenly blended.

∂ Put the watercress in a large mixing bowl along with the artichoke halves, walnuts, herbs, onions, chilies, and just a little sea salt and black pepper. Then break the feta roughly into 1in (2.5cm) chunks and mix all the ingredients together well. Slice the chicken breasts thinly, almost shredding them, add them to the salad, and toss lightly until all the ingredients are evenly distributed.

∂ Arrange the salad on a large, flat serving platter, then drizzle the dressing all over the salad before serving.

Fig & Green Bean Salad with Date Molasses & Toasted Almonds

Just when you thought pomegranate molasses was the new kid on the block, I throw you a date molasses curve ball. But, of course, molasses (a 100 percent concentrate of the pure juice of whichever ingredient it derives from) comes in many varieties—date, grape, mulberry, sumac, and sour cherry, for instance. The downside is that many of these are rather tricky to find, unless you live near a Middle Eastern grocery store or shop online.

SERVES 4

1lb (400g) fine green beans, trimmed

3 tbsp olive oil

1 tbsp red wine vinegar

2 tsp crushed sea salt flakes (less if using table salt)

3 tbsp date molasses

8 large black figs, quartered

2½oz (70g) flaked almonds, toasted

∂ **Tip**
Date molasses makes the perfect vinaigrette to complement this fig salad, but good-quality aged balsamic vinegar will also produce a fine result—just omit the red wine vinegar.

∂ Bring a large saucepan of water to a rapid boil over medium-high heat and cook the green beans for 5 minutes until they soften slightly but still retain their crunch. Drain them and immediately plunge them into a bowl of iced water or under a running cold tap to stop them overcooking. Once cool, drain well.

∂ To make the dressing, mix the oil, vinegar, sea salt, and date molasses together in a small bowl, stirring well to create a smooth dressing.

∂ Arrange the figs and beans on a large platter and drizzle over the dressing. Sprinkle the toasted flaked almonds on top before serving.

Fennel & Apple Salad with Dill & Pomegranate Seeds

This is the fennel dish that has converted many a fennel hater. The lemon dressing softens the aniseed flavor of fennel, and the sweetness of both the apple and pomegranate seeds makes this a delicate and refreshing accompaniment to a meal. As well as pretty to look at it is also packed with flavor, and the addition of dill gives life to every mouthful.

SERVES 6 AS A SIDE DISH

3 large fennel bulbs, trimmed of hard stalks and green skin removed

olive oil

juice of 2 lemons

2 nice, large apples

1 x ¾oz/20g packet of dill, leaves picked and roughly chopped

3½oz (100g) pomegranate seeds

sea salt

freshly ground black pepper

∂ Wash your fennel bulbs and quarter them. Using a sharp knife, shave or thinly slice each quarter and put the slices into a large mixing bowl. Drizzle with a good glug of olive oil and half the lemon juice and give it all a good mix to prevent the fennel going brown.

∂ Wash your apples and quarter them, removing the core and seeds as you do so. Thinly slice each quarter. Add the slices to the mixing bowl along with the chopped dill, pomegranate seeds, and remaining lemon juice. Toss the ingredients well to ensure everything is generously coated in the dressing, then season with sea salt and a little black pepper to taste.

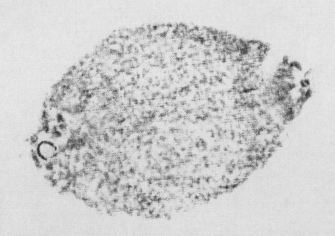

Shirazi Salad

Taking its name from the city of Shiraz in Iran (which is also the place from which the Shiraz grape gets its name), this dish is pretty much the national salad of Iran—if we actually had a national salad, of course. *Shirazi* is the most common accompaniment to most meals. Other versions include the Indian *kachumber* salad, Afghani salad, and Lebanese salad—all of which are almost identical. I like to add pomegranate seeds and a little sumac to give the salad a new dimension, but even without, it is incredibly refreshing and a firm favorite of mine.

SERVES 4–6

1 cucumber

6 ripe vine tomatoes, halved and cored

1 red onion

olive oil

3 pinches of sea salt

freshly ground black pepper

juice of 1 lemon

2 heaped tsp sumac

7oz (200g) pomegranate seeds

∂ Wash the cucumber and tomatoes. Finely dice the cucumber: the best way to do this is to halve your cucumber lengthways and cut each half into ½in- (1cm-) thick lengths. Slice each of these pieces lengthways into long thin strips about ¼in (5mm). Chop each of these strips widthways into small cubes, then put into a salad bowl.

∂ Finely dice the tomatoes by slicing each tomato half into 3, then cut each piece into ¼in (5mm) strips. Chop these into small cubes, as with the cucumber, and add to the bowl.

∂ Peel the red onion, removing any tough outer skins, and cut in half from the top down. Finely chop each half: slice off the bottom cores, then finely slice each half into ⅛in- (3mm-) thick half moons, then turn the onion around and cut ⅛in (3mm) "slices " at 90° to your existing slices to produce perfect, finely diced pieces of red onion. Add these to the bowl.

∂ Add a generous drizzle of olive oil to the mixture, just enough to lubricate it. Season with the sea salt and some black pepper, pour over the lemon juice, and give the ingredients a good mix to distribute the dressing evenly. At this point, you can sprinkle over the sumac and pomegranate seeds. Put the salad in the refrigerator for 20 minutes, since it is best served chilled.

Red Rice Salad with Barberries, Grilled Vegetables & Toasted Almonds

Camargue red rice is a fantastic ingredient in salads. It is wonderfully nutty and chewy and holds its texture so well that it makes the perfect carrier for lots of other ingredients and flavors. I like to dress the salad with a honey and orange vinaigrette that the rice absorbs, giving every grain a lovely flavor. What you put into this salad is up to you, but this is my favorite combination, using grilled vegetables, toasted whole almonds for crunch, and lovely tart barberries for little citric bursts of flavor in every mouthful. Serve with grilled fish or chicken, or as a meal in itself.

SERVES 6-8 AS A SIDE DISH

scant 1½ cups (½lb/250g) Camargue red rice

2 handfuls of dried barberries (or use unsweetened dried sour cherries or cranberries)

1 red onion, finely diced

good-quality olive oil

sea salt

freshly ground black pepper

juice of ½ orange

2 tbsp runny honey

3 tbsp red wine vinegar

1 large zucchini, sliced lengthways into ¼in- (5mm-) thick strips

1 large eggplant, cut into ½in- (1cm-) thick round slices

10½oz (300g) roasted red peppers in oil, drained and roughly diced

2 x ¾oz/20g packets of flat leaf parsley, leaves picked and finely chopped

1 x ¾oz/20g packet of cilantro, leaves picked and finely chopped

3½oz (100g) blanched whole almonds, toasted

∂ Cook the rice as per the package instructions. Rinse well in cold water and drain.

∂ Put the rice, barberries, and onion in a large mixing bowl and add enough olive oil to coat the rice well, a generous seasoning of sea salt and black pepper, the orange juice, honey, and vinegar. Set aside to allow the rice to soak in all the flavors while you prepare the vegetables.

∂ Preheat a griddle pan over medium heat. Brush the slices of zucchini with olive oil and grill them for 4–5 minutes, or until black griddle marks appear on each side. Transfer to a chopping board and set aside.

∂ Brush the eggplant slices with a more generous coating of olive oil and grill them in the griddle pan for approximately 8 minutes on each side until the texture softens and they are cooked through. Remove from the pan to a chopping board and set aside.

∂ Roughly chop the zucchini and cut the eggplant slices into cubes. Add to the rice along with the peppers, herbs, and toasted almonds and give the ingredients a good stir before serving.

Fattoush Salad

If you have ever been to a Lebanese restaurant, two salads always feature on the menu—*tabbouleh* and, of course, *fattoush*. While I love *tabbouleh*, *fattoush* feels more like a proper salad to me and has the added bonus of croutons or deep-fried pieces of bread. There is so much crunch to this salad and I believe that is what wins me over... plus the fact that the simple dressing cuts through a heavy Middle Eastern meal beautifully.

SERVES 6

2 (preferably stale) large pitas or *khobz* flatbreads (or any flatbread you like)

1lb (400g) cherry or baby plum tomatoes, roughly chopped

4 heads of little gem or romaine lettuce, halved lengthways and roughly chopped

1 large cucumber, halved lengthways and cut into ½in- (1cm-) thick half moons

1 red pepper, cored, deseeded, and cut into 1in (2.5cm) cubes

1 green pepper, cored, deseeded, and cut into 1in (2.5cm) cubes

7oz (200g) radishes, trimmed and cut into quarters

1 bunch of scallions, thinly sliced

1 x ¾oz/20g packet of flat leaf parsley, leaves picked and finely chopped

1 x ¾oz/20g packet of mint, leaves picked and finely chopped

1 heaped tbsp sumac, plus extra to garnish

5 tbsp olive oil

juice of 1½ lemons

sea salt

freshly ground black pepper

∂ Preheat the oven to 400°F/200°C. Line a baking sheet with parchment paper.

∂ Cut the flatbread roughly into 1½in (4cm) squares and lay them on the baking sheet. Toast them in the oven for 15 minutes, or until they are dry and completely crunchy.

∂ Put all the salad ingredients into a large salad or mixing bowl and sprinkle over the sumac, olive oil, lemon juice, and sea salt and black pepper to taste. Toss the salad well, ensuring everything gets a good coating of dressing. Serve it piled high, topped with the toasted croutons and an extra sprinkling of sumac.

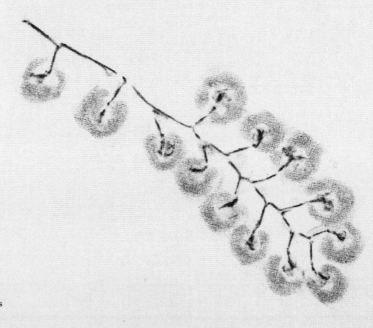

Chargrilled Eggplants with Saffron Yogurt, Parsley & Pickled Chilies

Eggplant is much loved and revered in Eastern culture and I especially love it chargrilled, which gives an added meatiness and smoky flavor. Saffron is the world's most expensive spice. The purest and highest grade of saffron comes from Iran and infusing some yogurt with its potency adds the perfect finish to grilled eggplants in my greedy, yet humble, opinion.

SERVES 4

2 large or 3 small eggplants, cut into ½in- (1cm-) thick slices

olive oil, for brushing

2 good pinches of saffron threads, ground with a mortar and pestle

2 tbsp boiling hot water

1 cup (250ml) Greek yogurt

2 tbsp garlic oil

sea salt

1 x ¾oz/20g packet of flat leaf parsley, leaves picked and roughly chopped

8 red pickled chilies, thinly sliced

1 tsp nigella seeds

∂ Preheat a griddle pan over medium-high heat. Brush the eggplant slices with olive oil on one side and chargrill them for approximately 6–8 minutes on each side, brushing the reverse side with more oil as you turn them over, until the texture softens and they are cooked through with nice griddle marks. Set aside.

∂ Using a mortar and pestle, grind the saffron to a powder, then pour over the boiling water and leave to infuse for at least 15 minutes. Once done, put the cooled saffron water into the yogurt, along with the garlic oil and a generous seasoning of sea salt, and mix well. If you want to slacken the yogurt mixture, stir in up to 5 tablespoons water.

∂ Arrange the eggplant slices on a platter, drizzle liberally with the saffron yogurt, scatter over the chopped parsley, and top with the thin slices of pickled chilies. Sprinkle with the nigella seeds and serve.

Spiced Root Vegetable Cakes with Tamarind & Date Sauce

Based on the Swiss potato rösti, this dish uses other root vegetables along with the potatoes, and the Middle Eastern spices transform it into something altogether more interesting. I like to serve the cakes with my tamarind and date sauce, which has a tangy sweet-and-sour character that makes the perfect accompaniment to the spiced cakes.

MAKES 14–16

1lb 2oz (500g) potatoes (I prefer waxy, but floury are also fine), scrubbed

1 bunch of scallions, thinly sliced

2 carrots, coarsely grated

1 parsnip, finely grated

1 large beet, finely grated

2 tsp ground cumin

2 tsp turmeric

2 tsp ground coriander

1 small bunch of cilantro, leaves picked and finely chopped, plus extra to garnish

2 small red chilies, finely chopped

2 large free-range eggs

2 tbsp all-purpose flour

sea salt and freshly ground black pepper

vegetable oil, for frying

For the Tamarind & Date Sauce

3½oz (100g) dates, pitted and roughly chopped

2½ tbsp (50g) tamarind paste

3 tbsp runny honey

1 tsp ground cumin

½ tsp ground ginger

1 tsp crushed sea salt flakes (less if using table salt)

squeeze of lemon juice

1⅔ cups (400ml) hot water

∂ Bring a large pan of salted water to a boil. Parboil your unpeeled potatoes for about 10–15 minutes (depending on their size). Using a skewer, pierce through a potato—the exterior should be cooked but the inside should still be a little hard. Drain the potatoes, place the pan in the sink, and run a cold tap over the potatoes until they cool down.

∂ To make the tamarind and date sauce, put the ingredients into a bowl and mix well, then blitz them in a blender or using a hand blender until the mixture is smooth. Preheat a small saucepan over medium heat, pour in the mixture, and bring to a gentle boil. Cook until the sauce has cooked through and become smooth. At this point, you can decide if you need a little more water to slacken the mixture, and if so, just add a little and cook for a further 5 minutes, then remove the pan from heat and set aside.

∂ Once the potatoes have cooled, drain and dry them and, without peeling the skins, grate them into a large mixing bowl. Add the remaining ingredients, except for the oil, and combine them well until you have an even mixture, well seasoned with salt and pepper.

∂ Preheat the oven to its lowest setting. Make little flat patties out of the mixture, each about 3in (7cm) in diameter.

∂ Preheat a large frying pan over medium heat and drizzle a good amount of oil into the pan. Fry several patties at a time without overcrowding the pan. The aim is to simply brown the cakes well on both sides, since the potato is pretty much cooked already—about 6–8 minutes on each side should do it. Keep the cooked batches warm in the oven while you fry the remaining patties.

∂ Serve with a generous drizzle of the date and tamarind sauce and a handful of chopped cilantro sprinkled over.

Persian *Kashk* Eggplants

Remember the nursery rhyme "Little Miss Muffet sat on her tuffet, eating her curds and whey"...? Well, whey is exactly what *kashk* is: a thick, almost cheese-like substance that is now pasteurized and sold in jars in Persian and Middle Eastern shops. I absolutely love the stuff. It is salty enough to make your lips tingle, but when you combine it with eggplants and fried onions, the result is a thing of beauty. When I first introduced this dish to my supper club, I was scared that people wouldn't like it but—much to my surprise—it is one of the most popular dishes I have ever put on my menus. Scoop it up with flatbread and I guarantee you it will be like nothing else you have ever tasted.

SERVES 6-8

vegetable oil

1lb 10oz (750g) white onions, cut in half and thinly sliced into ¼in- (5mm-) thick half moons

5 large eggplants

11¾oz (340g) Persian *kashk* (whey) (about ½ large jar), or labneh, or strained thick yogurt

sea salt

∂ In a large cooking pot over medium-high heat if using gas, or high heat if using electric, add a good 2in (5cm) oil. Once the oil is hot, put in your onion slivers and deep-fry until dark brown and crispy. They may even look burned, but this is fine, as long as they aren't completely blackened. Once they are really crispy, remove them carefully with a metal slotted spoon and drain on paper towel. Take the pan off the heat, but do not throw out the remaining oil.

∂ Remove the tops of the eggplants and peel them carefully using a small knife (tomato knives with a serrated edge are best for this job). Cut the eggplants into 1in- (2.5cm-) thick discs and roughly chop them into 1½in (4cm) cubes (you don't need to be exact here).

∂ Return the large pan to the stove over medium heat if using gas, or medium-high heat if using electric, and fry the eggplants pieces until they are cooked through. You may find they don't all fit, in which case, keep adding more and more pieces slowly to the pan, as the eggplants will halve in volume once they begin to soften. You will most likely need to add a generous amount of oil to prevent the eggplants from sticking to the bottom of the pan, but don't worry, as excess oil can later be drained from the finished eggplant mass. To speed up the cooking of the eggplants, cover the pot with a lid to allow them to part steam, but do

keep an eye on them and keep stirring and moving them every so often to prevent them from sticking to the pan too much. Eggplants contain sugar and some will, inevitably, stick to the pan, but this isn't a problem.

∂ Once the eggplants have softened fully and gained a little color, spoon off any excess oil, then break up some of the eggplant pieces with the back of a spoon so that some pieces are mashed and some are chunky. Don't worry if some pieces are not fully mashed—it's nice to have different textures. Reserving about 2 small handfuls of the fried onions, add the rest to the eggplant mixture and stir well, then add the *kashk* (whey) or yogurt, along with a few generous sprinklings of sea salt, and ensure everything has been well incorporated. Take this time to scrape off any eggplant matter that may be stuck to the bottom of the pan and incorporate it into the mixture.

∂ Reduce the heat to a low flame on gas, or a medium temperature on electric and cook the mixture slowly for 1½ hours, or until it changes from the creamy white mixture that it was when the *kashk* was added, to an intense khaki color. Remove the pan from the heat and serve the dish with a generous garnish of the reserved crispy fried onions.

Cumin-Roasted Carrots with Honey-Lemon Dressing & Goat Cheese

Every time I bought a bag of carrots, I found myself left with more than half the bag, so I came up with a way to turn a few straggly carrots into a really satisfying side dish or even a main meal. I like using cumin seeds with carrots, and the honey-lemon dressing enhances their natural sweetness. The goat cheese melts slightly after a few minutes, making each mouthful wonderfully creamy and delicious. Who needs meat when vegetables taste this good?

SERVES 4–6

1lb 10oz (750g) carrots, cut diagonally into 1in- (2.5cm-) thick slices

olive oil

1½ heaped tbsp cumin seeds

sea salt

freshly ground black pepper

juice of 1 lemon

3 tbsp runny honey

3½oz (100g) soft goat cheese (chèvre)

1 bunch of dill, leaves picked and roughly chopped

good sprinkling of nigella seeds

∂ Preheat the oven to 400°F/200°C. Line a large baking sheet with parchment paper.

∂ Place the carrot pieces on the baking sheet and drizzle with a good amount of olive oil. Sprinkle over the cumin seeds, season well with sea salt and black pepper, and, using your hands, give everything a thorough mix to ensure the cumin, oil, and seasoning evenly coats the roots. Roast for 25–30 minutes, or until the carrots are cooked through.

∂ Mix the lemon juice and honey together until evenly dissolved. Remove the carrots from the oven, drizzle the honey-lemon dressing over them, and carefully toss them (using appropriate utensils) to ensure the dressing coats the carrots well. Roast for a further 8–10 minutes, or until the carrots are slightly sticky.

∂ Remove the carrots from the oven and arrange them on a flat plate. Crumble the goat cheese liberally over the roots, then sprinkle the chopped dill over them, followed by the nigella seeds.

Harissa-Marinated Asparagus

Nothing beats asparagus in season and, paired with spicy harissa and zingy lemon, they make the perfect accompaniment to grilled meat, fish, and haloumi.

<u>SERVES 2</u>

2 tbsp olive oil

2 tsp harissa paste

2 tbsp runny honey

zest and juice of 1 lemon

2 pinches of sea salt

½lb (250g) asparagus spears, trimmed

∂ Put the olive oil, harissa, honey, lemon zest and juice, and sea salt in a small bowl and mix really well until the honey has dissolved fully into the mixture.

∂ Place the asparagus in a shallow dish and pour over the marinade. Using your hands (you can wear plastic gloves, if you wish), coat each asparagus spear in the marinade, then cover the dish with plastic wrap, and allow the asparagus to marinate at room temperature for 30 minutes—but for no more than an hour.

∂ Preheat a large heavy-based frying pan—or a griddle pan, if you prefer—over medium-high heat and pan-fry the asparagus for 8–10 minutes, allowing 4–5 minutes per side. Serve hot, or cold as part of a salad.

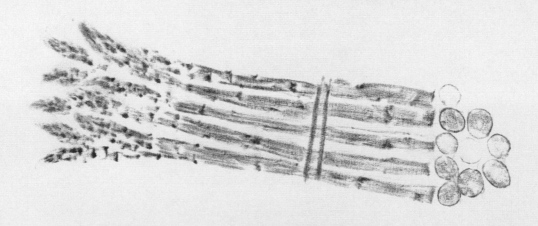

Tray-Roasted Baby Zucchinis with Garlic & Tomato

I often struggle to think of interesting things to do with zucchini. Often I use them grated in quiches and vegetable fritters, but roasting vegetables always makes life so much easier. You put everything into a roasting pan, season well, drizzle on some olive oil, throw it in the oven and you're done! If, however, you add some tomato, garlic, and just a little spice, the vegetables come alive and are no longer a side dish but rather more of a main event.

SERVES 6–8 AS A SIDE DISH

1lb 5oz (600g) baby zucchinis

1 garlic bulb, cloves peeled and thinly sliced

6 large ripe tomatoes, each cored and cut into 8 pieces

olive oil

1 tsp ground cumin

sea salt

freshly ground black pepper

∂ Preheat the oven to 400°F/200°C. Line a baking sheet with parchment paper.

∂ Place the baby zucchinis onto the prepared baking sheet, scatter over the garlic slices, then squeeze the tomato pieces a little as you scatter them over the zucchinis, too. Drizzle with olive oil and sprinkle on the cumin and a good seasoning of sea salt and black pepper.

∂ Roast the zucchinis for 15 minutes, or until they are cooked through. Serve immediately.

Butternut Squash with Pistachio, Pesto, Feta & Pomegranate Seeds

Middle Eastern people often perceive butternut squash as bland. Taking inspiration from an Asian pesto-and-squash dish made by my friend, the chef Tony Singh, I came up with my own Persian pistachio pesto, adding salty crumbled feta cheese and a handful of vibrant pomegranate seeds for a burst of flavor. The result? It has become one of my most popular supper club dishes of all time and has proven itself to be the dish that converts those who were formerly not the greatest of squash fans.

SERVES 2 AS A MAIN COURSE OR 4 AS A SIDE DISH

1 large butternut squash, quartered lengthways and deseeded

4 tbsp olive oil

sea salt

freshly ground black pepper

5¼oz (150g) feta cheese

3½oz (100g) pomegranate seeds

For the pesto

3½oz (100g) shelled pistachios

2½oz (70g) Parmesan or Grana Padano cheese, chopped into rough chunks

olive oil

1 small bunch of cilantro, leaves picked

1 small bunch of parsley, leaves picked

1 small bunch of dill, leaves picked

3 tbsp chili oil

juice of 1 lemon

∂ In a food processor, blitz the pistachios and cheese together, adding a generous amount of olive oil to slacken the mixture. Put all the herbs into the food processor with a little more olive oil, as well as the chili oil and lemon juice, and blitz again, then add some crushed sea salt and give the mixture one last whizz. Taste the pesto, ensuring it has enough salt and acidity, then allow it to rest in the refrigerator until you need it.

∂ Preheat the oven to 400°F/200°C. Once the oven is hot, rub each wedge of butternut squash with the oil, season generously with sea salt and black pepper, and place it on a baking sheet lined with parchment paper. Roast the squash for about 45–50 minutes, or just until the edges have begun to char slightly. You want to blacken the edges a little—this gives them a nice chewy texture. To check the squash to see if it is properly cooked, insert a knife into the flesh—if it slides clean through, the squash is ready. If you feel resistance, return the squash to the oven for a few more minutes.

∂ Serve each wedge of butternut squash on a plate, drizzled generously with the vibrant green pesto. Crumble the feta cheese on top and scatter over the pomegranate seeds to finish.

Turmeric & Cumin Roasted Potatoes

Potatoes aren't very common in Middle Eastern dishes, and when they are used we don't usually serve them as a side dish as it is generally done in the West. I created this dish for guests using a heavy-handed amount of spicing that surprisingly worked really well. It is a fantastic accompaniment to grilled meat, poultry, and fish, as the potatoes can really hold a lot more spicing than even I had initially given them credit for. Use the leftovers to make a potato salad the next day, or fry them with eggs to make an Eastern-style Spanish omelet.

SERVES 4-6 AS A SIDE DISH

1lb 10oz (750g) baby potatoes, scrubbed

4 tbsp olive oil

2 heaped tsp turmeric

3 heaped tsp ground cumin

1 tsp cayenne pepper

3 tsp crushed sea salt flakes (less if using table salt)

freshly ground black pepper

chopped fresh herbs and crumbled feta, to serve (optional)

∂ Preheat the oven to 400°F/200°C. Line a large baking tray with parchment paper.

∂ Halve the potatoes. If you are using a larger variety of potato, cut them into rough ¾in (2cm) cubes. Ensure all the pieces are roughly the same size (there's no need to be too obsessive about this) so that they cook evenly.

∂ Place the potatoes onto the prepared baking tray and drizzle the olive oil over them. Sprinkle on the turmeric, cumin, cayenne pepper, sea salt, and a generous amount of black pepper and, using your hands, mix everything together, ensuring the potatoes are evenly coated in the oil and spice mixture. Spread out the potatoes in a single layer so that they roast properly, then roast for 45 minutes, or until they are nicely golden brown. Keep in mind that the spice blend will have colored the potatoes, so once done, they may be a deeper brown than you are expecting.

∂ Serve with meat or chicken, or crumble over a little feta and some fresh herbs of your choice to make this dish a meal in itself.

Roasted Garlic & Sweet Potato Purée

I would choose sweet potatoes over regular potatoes any day. Roasted, fried, or mashed, they are light, sweet, and totally delicious. This recipe allows you to add a little flavor, which, for the sake of variety, is a good option. Although I love the natural flavor of sweet potatoes with just a little sea salt, roasted garlic imparts a mellow flavor to the sweet flesh that makes it delicious. I prefer to serve this dish alongside lamb dishes—I find the combination so satisfying—although I have also been known to dip toasted ciabatta into it and eat it as a warm dip.

SERVES 4

6 large sweet potatoes (skin on)

4 fat garlic cloves, unpeeled

olive oil, for drizzling

½ tsp ground cinnamon

sea salt

freshly ground black pepper

2 tbsp (25g) butter

pomegranate molasses, to serve

∂ Preheat the oven to 350°F/180°C. Roast the sweet potatoes whole for 1 hour, or until cooked through.

∂ Place the unpeeled garlic cloves on a double layer of foil, drizzle with a little olive oil, then seal the foil around them. Roast for 30–35 minutes, or until the cloves are soft and squishy.

∂ Once the sweet potatoes are cooked, allow them to cool slightly—just enough to allow you to handle them—and scoop out the flesh into a saucepan set over low heat.

∂ Peel the roasted garlic cloves and mash them into the sweet potatoes, along with the cinnamon and some salt and pepper to taste. Cook the purée for a further 6–8 minutes, stirring it to prevent the mixture from sticking. Finish with the butter, stirring well to incorporate it and make the purée nice and smooth. Serve with a little drizzle of pomegranate molasses.

Za'atar Roasted Squash with Spiced Yogurt & Pickled Chilies

Once again, demonstrating the versatility of za'atar, I've mixed this winning spice blend with oil to make a paste that is rubbed over butternut squash just before roasting it in the oven. Combined with a lovely spiced yogurt, fiery pickled chilies, and a scattering of fresh parsley, the humble butternut squash is transformed from a supporting act into a star attraction. It's perfect for vegetarians and meat-lovers alike, as it satisfies on every level.

SERVES 4 AS A SIDE DISH

1 large butternut squash

3 tbsp za'atar

3 tbsp olive oil

sea salt

For the Spiced Yogurt Sauce

1 cup (200g) Greek yogurt

1 bunch of mint, leaves picked and finely chopped

2 tsp sumac

1 tbsp ground coriander

2 tbsp olive oil

zest and juice of 1 lemon

freshly ground black pepper

To serve

1 small bunch of flat leaf parsley, leaves picked and roughly chopped

2 tsp nigella seeds

8 fat red pickled chilies, thinly sliced

∂ Preheat the oven to 450°F/240°C. Line a baking sheet with parchment paper.

∂ Cut the squash horizontally in half at the point of the bulge. Now halve each portion vertically. Scoop out the seeds with a metal spoon and discard, then halve each piece vertically again until you have 8 pieces. Peel the squash and cut the pieces into any shape you wish.

∂ Make a paste with the za'atar and olive oil in a small bowl and rub the squash pieces all over with paste until every piece is well coated. Place all the pieces onto the prepared baking sheet. Season with sea salt, then roast for about 40–45 minutes (depending on the size of the pieces of squash), or until the edges start to brown and almost char a little.

∂ Meanwhile, in another bowl, mix the yogurt with the fresh mint, sumac, coriander, olive oil, lemon zest and juice, and sea salt and black pepper to taste. Mix the ingredients together well, then taste and adjust the seasoning if necessary.

∂ Remove the squash pieces from the oven and place them on a serving platter. Liberally dollop or pour the yogurt over the wedges, then sprinkle with the parsley. Follow this with a scant scattering of nigella seeds. Lastly, scatter over the pickled chilies. Serve this dish alongside meat, fish, or even grilled haloumi.

Desserts & sweet treats

Spiced Carrot, Pistachio & Almond Cake with Rosewater Cream

I am not the most natural of bakers, so I work hard to perfect foolproof, crowd-pleasing recipes that work well with my style of cooking. Iran has a huge nut-producing trade and pistachios are the king of Persian nuts. I first made this cake when I started doing supper clubs because we don't really have desserts in Iran and I knew my diners would expect a proper dessert, so this cake was born… and the rest (as they say) is history.

SERVES 10

3 large free-range eggs

1 cup (7oz/200g) superfine sugar

2 tsp vanilla extract

7oz (200g) ground almonds

3½oz (100g) unsweetened shredded coconut

2 heaped tsp ground cinnamon

11 tbsp (150g) unsalted butter, melted

2 large carrots, coarsely grated

3½oz (100g) shelled pistachios, roughly chopped

confectioners' sugar, for dusting

For the Rosewater Cream

1¼ cups (300ml) heavy whipping cream

2–3 tbsp rosewater

3–4 tbsp confectioners' sugar

a few chopped pistachios

∂ Preheat the oven to 320°F/160°C. Line a 9in (23cm) springform cake pan with enough parchment paper to cover the base and sides. You won't need to grease the pan or the paper, since the oils from the nuts and butter in the batter prevent the cake from sticking to the paper.

∂ Beat the eggs, sugar, and vanilla extract together in a mixing bowl. Add the ground almonds, coconut, and cinnamon and stir, then add the melted butter and give the ingredients a thorough mix. Add the grated carrots and pistachios and mix again until the ingredients are evenly blended, then gently pour or spoon the batter into your prepared cake pan and bake for 1 hour, or until it feels firm to touch and a crust forms on top. Check the cake at 40 minutes to ensure it is cooking evenly. Once cooked, allow to cool in the pan, overnight if you can wait; the cake is much moister once cooled and tastes better as a result.

∂ To make the rosewater cream, whip the cream along with the rosewater and confectioners' sugar, either by hand or using an electric hand mixer, until the cream is thick and unctuous. Dollop a generous spoonful on the side of a slice of the cake and dust the cake and cream lightly with confectioners' sugar. Top with some chopped pistachios. I store this cake on a plate covered with plastic wrap and find it can be kept like this for up to 1 week.

Baklava

We don't really do dessert in the Middle East. We do tea... tea and *baklava*. The origins of *baklava* are not well documented and many countries have their own versions of this syrup-soaked treat. Greeks like using walnuts in theirs, Arabs use cashews and other nuts, Turks predominantly use pistachios and hazelnuts, and Persians use almonds and pistachios. Some add spices and some don't. In my version, I like to add a little zesty citrus kick to cut through the sweetness. We always serve *baklava* with black tea.

SERVES 8-10

10½oz (300g) ground almonds

3½oz (100g) slivered or blanched pistachios

½ cup (3½oz/100g) superfine sugar

zest of 2 oranges

zest of 1 lime

seeds from 6 green cardamom pods, ground with a mortar and pestle

pinch of ground cinnamon

11 tbsp (150g) unsalted butter, melted

2 packets of filo pastry (12 sheets)

For the syrup

generous ¾ cup (200ml) water

1 tbsp lemon juice

1½ cups (10½oz/300g) superfine sugar

∂ Combine the ground almonds, pistachios, sugar, and orange and lime zests in a mixing bowl with the ground cardamom seeds and cinnamon. Set aside.

∂ Preheat the oven to 350°F/180°C.

∂ Select a 10–12in (25–30cm) square ovenproof dish and brush the base well with melted butter. Line the base of the dish with 6 sheets of filo pastry (keep the rest covered or they will dry out). Ensure there is enough of the pastry overhanging the edges of the dish to allow you to fold it over the contents of the dish later, when it comes to sealing the *baklava*. Brush the exposed base of the pastry generously with melted butter, then add the nut mixture into the base and flatten it gently to lightly compress the mixture. Use 5 of the remaining 6 sheets of filo pastry to top the nut mixture as evenly and neatly as possible, then tuck in the loose flaps from the bottom layers. Add the final sheet of pastry on top to seal the *baklava*. Brush the top layer generously with more melted butter.

∂ Using a very sharp knife, carefully cut straight or diagonal lines across the top layers of pastry. Bake for 25–30 minutes, or until the pastry is golden brown.

∂ Meanwhile, make the syrup. Put the water and lemon juice into a saucepan set over low-medium heat and dissolve the sugar in the mixture, stirring occasionally, until the liquid begins to thicken to a syrup consistency. This should take 20–25 minutes.

∂ Remove the *baklava* from the oven and immediately drizzle the syrup over the pastry. Allow it to seep into all the cuts that you made before baking. Allow to cool completely in the pan before cutting.

Lacy Saffron Fritters with Pistachio & Dill Sugar
Zoolbia

These lacy yogurt-based fritters are the perfect way to end a meal with some Persian black tea. Usually soaked in a heavy syrup, I prefer a lighter dill-and-pistachio sugar that makes them so much less sickly sweet and more addictive than anything. If dill is not your cup of tea, you can use basil or mint, but dill creates a subtle background flavor that works well in the crunchy sugar dusting.

MAKES ABOUT 16

¼ cup (6oz/175g) all-purpose flour

pinch of salt

1 x ¼oz/7g envelope active dry yeast

1 cup (250ml) warm water

generous ⅓ cup (75g) Greek yogurt

pinch of saffron threads, ground with a mortar and pestle, then dissolved in 2 tbsp boiling water

generous 2 cups (500ml) vegetable oil

For the Pistachio & Dill Sugar

2½oz (70g) shelled pistachios

good handful of dill, leaves picked and finely chopped

¾ cup (5¼oz/150g) superfine sugar

∂ Sift the flour into a mixing bowl and add the salt and yeast. Pour in the warm water and yogurt and mix well until you have a thick batter. Add the saffron water and stir until the batter takes on a lovely pale lemon color. Cover the bowl with plastic wrap and leave the batter to rest at room temperature for a couple of hours.

∂ Blitz the pistachios with the dill in a food processor until they are finely ground. In a small bowl, mix the resulting paste with the sugar, using a fork to break down any clusters, until you have an even pale green sugar. Keep it in an airtight container until you are ready to dust the fritters.

∂ Heat the vegetable oil on a large saucepan, but do not let it smoke. To check if the oil is hot enough for deep-frying, put in a drop of the batter, and if it sizzles within a couple of seconds, the oil is ready. I like to use squeezy bottles to drop the batter into the pan, although you can use a pastry bag with a narrow tip or spoon in the mixture to make free-form fritters. It doesn't matter how they look; as long as they aren't too thick or burned, they will taste great.

∂ Pipe the first fritter into the oil, moving quickly to create a small lacy pattern (keep it small, as the fritter will expand as it cooks). Test-fry it for about 1½ minutes, at which point you can flip it over (carefully) using a metal fork and fry for another 30 seconds or so, just to even out the color. Remove and drain the fritter onto a plate lined with paper towel. Repeat the process, but this time pipe 2–3 fritters into the oil at once, until the batter is used up and all the fritters are cooked. Dust each fritter with a little scattering of the dusting sugar and serve immediately.

Pistachio & Lemon Shortbreads

Whoever invented shortbread is a god in my eyes. The best I ever tasted was in Scotland and I have not had any since that could match its superb texture and taste. But that hasn't put me off making them at home. Being Persian, I have a natural inclination to throw pistachios into absolutely everything. In this dish, I combine them with a little lemon zest and some fragrant vanilla to make these lovely little giveaways for lucky recipients.

MAKES 18–20

3½oz (100g) shelled pistachios

⅓ cup (1¾oz/50g) rice flour

1¾ cups (½lb/250g) all-purpose flour

zest of 2 lemons

2 tsp vanilla bean paste

scant 1 cup (3½oz/100g) confectioners' sugar, sifted

½ tsp salt

14 tbsp (200g) unsalted butter, softened

olive oil

granulated sugar, for dusting

∂ Blitz the pistachios in a food processor roughly until they are broken down, but not too finely, since you want to retain crunch and texture.

∂ In a large mixing bowl, combine the pistachios with the ground rice, flour, lemon zest, vanilla paste, confectioners' sugar, and salt then work the butter into the mixture until a dough forms. Mix in just enough olive oil to help you form the dough into a solid ball, then roll the dough into a log about 1½–2in (4–5cm) wide. Wrap it tightly in plastic wrap, twisting the ends (like a candy wrapper) to achieve maximum tightness, then refrigerate for at least 1 hour.

∂ Preheat the oven to 300°F/150°C. Line a large baking sheet with parchment paper. Once the oven is hot, remove the dough from the refrigerator and cut it into ½in- (1cm-) thick discs. Lay these onto the paper-lined baking sheet, leaving a gap of ¾in (2cm) between each disc. Sprinkle some granulated sugar liberally over the tops of the discs, then bake for 20 minutes, or until the edges begin to turn slightly golden but the cookies themselves remain virtually the same color as they were prior to baking. Allow to cool completely on a wire rack before eating.

Strawberry & Pineapple Carpaccio with Basil & Mint Sugars

Fruit is one of the most popular options after a rich and decadent meal. Inspired by Jamie Oliver's recipe for pineapple carpaccio, I now make all kinds of herb or spice-flavored sugars to go with many different fruits. I especially like basil with berries, and strawberries and pineapple always seem the favorite among my diners and friends.

SERVES 4

1 large pineapple

1lb (400g) strawberries

generous handful of mint leaves, roughly chopped

3 tbsp sugar

generous handful of basil leaves, roughly chopped

∂ Cut the ends off the pineapple, ensuring you have a nice flat, sturdy base. Now cut away the pineapple skin using a sharp knife, starting at the top and sliding the knife down to the base. Cut in deep enough to remove any of the brown eyes around the flesh. Once peeled, halve the pineapple lengthways, then cut it lengthways again to make 4 quarters. There is a hard core in the center of the pineapple that you will need to cut away, so lay each quarter on its side and cut away and discard about ½in (1cm) of the inner core. While the quarter is laying flat in the same position, cut wafer-thin slices of pineapple until all 4 quarters are sliced. Set aside.

∂ Remove the green tops from the strawberries and then, using a small sharp knife, cut each berry into thin slices.

∂ To make the herb sugars, put the chopped mint in a mortar with half the sugar and, using the pestle, grind down the leaves with the sugar until the sugar turns green. Decant the mint sugar, then repeat the process with the basil and remaining sugar.

∂ Arrange the fruit onto a large platter (or divide it across individual platters, if preferred). Sprinkle the mint sugar over the pineapple carpaccio and the basil sugar over the strawberry carpaccio. Serve immediately.

Cinnamon & Citrus Almond Pastry Cigars

These crispy filo rolls make a great dessert or simple sweet treat. The filling is delicately spiced and perfumed with citrus zest to cleanse the palate. It's my take on a classic Moroccan Berber recipe for *m'hencha*, meaning "coiled like a snake." I love *m'hencha*, but making these pastry cigars is infinitely less tricky. They are kind of like *baklava*, but minus the heavy syrup and excess butter, and utterly addictive.

SERVES 12

7oz (200g) ground almonds

generous ½ cup (4½oz/125g) sugar

2 tbsp rosewater

1 tbsp orange extract

zest of 2 oranges

zest of 2 limes

1½ heaped tsp ground cinnamon

7 tbsp (100g) butter, melted

6 sheets (1 packet) of filo pastry

confectioners' sugar, for dusting

∂ **Tip**

Make the almond paste mixture in advance and keep it in the fridge or freezer until you are ready to use it.

∂ Preheat the oven to 400°F/200°C (preferably fan assisted for this recipe). Line a baking sheet with parchment paper.

∂ Combine the ground almonds, sugar, rosewater, orange extract, citrus zests, cinnamon, and 1¾oz (50g) of the melted butter in a bowl until they form a thick paste.

∂ Cut each of your 6 sheets of pastry in half and place them horizontally in front of you. Divide the almond paste into 12 equal portions. Shape one portion into a ¾in (2cm) sausage shape about 3½in (9cm) long and place it along the bottom edge of the pastry. Fold the bottom corners of the pastry up over the filling, then roll up the pastry from the bottom, tucking in the sides as you go. Brush the remaining flap of pastry with some of the leftover melted butter and finish rolling to secure.

∂ Repeat this process until all 12 cigars are rolled, then place them on the prepared baking sheet. Brush the cigars all over with melted butter, then bake for 20–25 minutes, or until golden brown. Remove from oven and allow to cool slightly, then dust with confectioners' sugar and serve.

Eastern Mess

Having spent almost all of my life in England, I am no stranger to the quintessentially British dessert, Eton Mess. I like to believe that it was first created as a happy accident in a failed attempt at strawberry pavlova at Eton College, although this is largely believed to be a myth. Over the years, I have made versions using every fruit imaginable and have added a variety of flavors to the cream. I don't mind admitting that some were less successful than others. This version is perfumed with Persian rosewater and combined with raspberries, basil, and delicate slivered pistachios, which give a little crunch to every bite.

SERVES 6

2½ cups (600ml) heavy whipping cream

3 tbsp confectioners' sugar

1 tsp vanilla bean paste or the seeds scraped from 1 vanilla pod

2 tbsp rosewater

6 ready-made meringue cookies

1lb (450g) raspberries

handful of Greek basil leaves or torn basil leaves

2¾oz (75g) slivered or chopped pistachios

For the Raspberry Sauce

½lb (225g) raspberries

1 tbsp confectioners' sugar (you may need more if using raspberries out of season)

1 tbsp rosewater

squeeze of lemon juice

∂ Using an electric hand mixer, whip the cream, confectioners' sugar, vanilla paste or seeds, and rosewater together in a mixing bowl until soft peaks form. You don't want the cream to be too loose or too stiff, so keep an eye on the consistency. With the mixer set on a high speed, it should take about 3 minutes or so.

∂ To make the sauce, mash the the raspberries to a purée with the confectioners' sugar, rosewater, and lemon juice in a bowl until the mixture is completely smooth. Pass the mixture through a sieve to remove the raspberry seeds.

∂ Choose either a large platter or individual serving dishes. Now layer the cream, meringues, and raspberries in the serving dish(es), drizzling on the sauce and scattering over the basil leaves and pistachios as you go. Decorate the top layer with a little drizzle of sauce and a final scattering of basil leaves and pistachios. Serve immediately.

Cardamom & Rosewater Poached Pears

This dessert is simple, elegant, and the perfect light dessert to serve after a dinner of many dishes. The pears infuse in the heavenly scent of Persian rosewater and cardamom while poaching, which makes for a very decadent dessert. I have converted many a hater of cardamom with this dish.

SERVES 6

1⅔ cups (400ml) rosewater

12–16 cardamom pods, bruised or crushed a little

1½ cups (10½oz/300g) sugar

6 smooth-skinned pears, preferably nice big ones

chopped pistachios, for scattering

∂ Fill a large saucepan almost to the brim with boiling water and bring to a boil over medium-high heat. Add the rosewater, crushed cardamom pods, and sugar, reduce the heat, and simmer gently for 20 minutes.

∂ Peel the pears carefully, leaving the stems intact. Remove the cores from the bases of the pears using a small sharp knife. Place the peeled and cored pears upright in the poaching liquid and poach for 30–35 minutes, or until tender—you should be able to pierce them with a toothpick with no resistance. Remove the pears from the poaching liquid and set aside.

∂ Serve warm with a little of the poaching liquid and a scattering of chopped pistachios. I sometimes like to serve the pears on a bed of fresh pink rose petals (using thoroughly washed roses) to really capture the traditional Middle Eastern aromas. These pears are also good with vanilla ice cream.

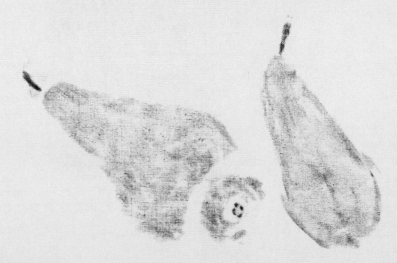

Pistachio, Honey & Orange Blossom Ice Cream

There is something wonderful about the process of making ice cream, especially when there is an ice cream maker involved. It makes life so easy and I am always astounded at how simple the process is. This particular ice cream captures all the flavors of the Middle East beautifully and is sweet and delicately floral, with notes of orange blossom. The crunch of pistachios is delightful. What's not to love? Served with or without a cone or—even better—wedged into a sweet brioche for the ultimate ice cream sandwich, this is heaven.

SERVES 4–6

7oz (200g) slivered pistachios, plus extra to decorate

¾ cup (5¼oz/150g) superfine sugar

2½ cups (600ml) whole milk

2½ cups (600ml) heavy cream

3 tbsp runny honey

generous ¾ cup (200ml) orange blossom water

1⅔ cups (400ml) unsweetened evaporated milk

zest of 2 oranges

∂ Blitz about three-quarters (5¼oz/150g) of the pistachios along with the sugar in a food processor until finely ground.

∂ Put the milk into a saucepan, add the cream, honey, orange blossom water, and the pistachio mixture and bring to a gentle boil. Over a period of 20–25 minutes, reduce the liquid by a quarter, stirring regularly to prevent it from bubbling over. The more you stir, the more the pistachios will release their oils and flavor into the ice cream base. Set aside to allow the mixture to cool.

∂ Pour the evaporated milk into the pistachio-cream mixture and stir in the grated orange zest and the remaining slivered pistachios. Mix well, then chill in the refrigerator for at least 2 hours or overnight.

∂ Once chilled, pour the mixture into an ice cream maker and churn for 25–30 minutes (or according to your manufacturer's instructions). Alternatively, pour the mixture into a large shallow container and freeze for 2 hours. Remove the container from the freezer and fork through the mixture to break down the ice crystals, then freeze again until firm. Serve in scoops with a sprinking of slivered pistachios.

Pistachio, Rose & Raspberry Madeleines

The thing about madeleines is that they should ideally be served still warm from the oven, which gives them a melt-in-the-mouth quality that makes them highly addictive. If you can stop after eating just one madeleine, then, believe me, you haven't had a good madeleine yet. These are perfumed with the scent of Persian roses, nutty with pistachios, and topped with a raspberry for a little juicy burst. I defy you to not scarf at least three of them in a row.

MAKES 30

3 large free-range eggs

scant 1 cup (6oz/175g) sugar

¼ cup (6oz/175g) all-purpose flour

2 tsp (¼oz/ 10g) baking powder

pinch of salt

14 tablespoons (200g) unsalted butter, melted and cooled, plus 3½ tbsp (50g) extra, softened, for greasing

3 tbsp runny honey

4 tbsp rosewater

5¼oz (150g) shelled pistachios, finely chopped

30 raspberries (1 per madeleine)

∂ Crack the eggs into a large mixing bowl, add the sugar, and beat until pale and fluffy. In a separate bowl, combine the flour, baking powder, and salt and set aside. Mix the cooled melted butter with the honey and rosewater and pour this into the egg-sugar mixture. Stir until the mixture is smooth.

∂ Add the chopped pistachios to the wet ingredients and stir in well. Lastly, incorporate half of the flour into the mixture, give it a vigorous stir, then add the remaining flour, and stir until all the flour is evenly combined. Cover the bowl with plastic wrap and refrigerate for at least 2 hours, or overnight if preferred.

∂ Once you are ready to bake, preheat the oven to 375°F/190°C. Brush each mold in a 12-shell madeleine pan with softened butter and place it in the freezer to harden for a few minutes, then brush again with softened butter. Put 1 heaped tablespoon of the batter into each mold. You won't use up all the batter at once, so refrigerate the rest of the batter until the first batch is cooked. Push a single raspberry into the batter in the center of each mold. Bake for 5 minutes, turn the oven off for 1 minute, then set the oven to 320°F/160°C and bake for a further 5 minutes, or until they are golden all over.

∂ Remove the madeleines from the oven and turn them out (a teaspoon will help you to pop them out of their molds). Wash the madeline pan and repeat the process until the rest of the batter is used up. Serve the madeleines hot from the oven, although they can be kept for 48 hours in an airtight container—but bear in mind that they always taste best freshly baked.

Rice Pudding

We call rice pudding *sheer berenj*, meaning "milky rice." Although I was never very fond of it as a child, I have rediscovered it as an adult and have added my own flavors to it to create something that makes me happy and fills me with all the comfort that a good rice pudding should provide. I like adding citrus rind to my cooking—it gives things a zesty scent and flavor without the acidity. And nuts give this dish a lovely crunch.

SERVES 4-6

2¾ cups (650ml) whole milk

generous ¾ cup (200ml) heavy cream

2 tsp rosewater

4 green cardamom pods, crushed, seeds ground with a mortar and pestle

1 tsp vanilla bean paste or the seeds scraped from 1 vanilla pod

2 tbsp runny honey, plus extra for drizzling

scant 1 cup (7oz/200g) short-grain white rice

3½ tbsp (50g) unsalted butter

zest of 1 lime

To serve

1¾oz (50g) flaked almonds, toasted

1¾oz (50g) chopped shelled pistachios

handful of dried edible rose petals

∂ Set a large saucepan over medium-low heat, pour in the milk, cream, rosewater, ground cardamom seeds, vanilla paste or seeds, and the honey, and stir well until the vanilla paste has dissolved into the liquid evenly. Without allowing the contents to boil, heat up the liquid, then increase the heat to medium and add the rice.

∂ Once the rice is in, you will need to stir the mixture continuously for about 20 minutes or so to draw out the starch, which will enrich the dish. Should the rice dry out a little during the cooking process, add a little more milk.

∂ Once the rice is cooked, add the butter and stir well until it melts. Turn off the heat and stir in the lime zest to give the dish a burst of freshness.

∂ In the Middle East, although we do occasionally eat rice puddings hot, we love to eat them chilled. So decant the pudding either into a large serving dish or as individual portions, decorate generously with the almonds and pistachios, scatter on a few dried rose petals, and refrigerate for a couple of hours. Drizzle over a little honey just before serving.

Syrup-Poached Apricots with Walnuts & Clotted Cream

Kaymak is a bit of an obsession in Turkey. Everywhere you go, there is *kaymak*: *kaymak* ice cream, yogurt, cakes, and sweet treats filled with *kaymak*... so I found myself asking what on earth is this *kaymak* stuff? The answer is simple... it is clotted cream and Turks love it. This is my version of a popular treat enjoyed by Turks, made with dried apricots stuffed with clotted cream and walnuts. They are perfect mouthfuls of deliciousness and look so pretty. Although they are very sweet and rich, when paired with a nice cup of black tea or mint tea, they are a naughty treat that's well worth indulging in.

SERVES 6

generous 2 cups (500ml) water

6 tbsp superfine sugar

1 vanilla pod, split down the center

2 strips of lemon zest

squeeze of lemon juice

1 cinnamon stick (about 3in/7cm long)

1 tbsp green cardamom pods, lightly cracked

24 dried apricots (about 7oz/200g)

7oz (200g) clotted cream (see tip to make your own)

about 7oz (200g) walnut halves (1 per apricot)

∂ **Tip**
To make homemade clotted cream, pour 4¼ cups (1 liter) heavy cream into a shallow ovenproof dish and place in a preheated oven at 200°F/90°C for 2 hours. Cool, then chill in the refrigerator for 24 hours until a crust forms on the surface.

∂ Set a large saucepan over medium heat, pour in the water, add the sugar, and stir until the sugar dissolves. Add the vanilla pod, lemon zest and juice, cinnamon stick, and cardamom pods and reduce the heat to low-medium. Simmer gently for about 15 minutes.

∂ Add the apricots to the syrup and poach them for 15 minutes, then switch off the heat and leave the apricots in the poaching syrup until they are cool. At this stage, I like to put the clotted cream into the freezer briefly (for about 15 minutes, just until you need to use it), which makes it much easier to cleanly fill the apricots.

∂ Once the apricots are cool, pour a little hot water into a cup to have ready for rinsing your teaspoon during the filling process.

∂ Remove an apricot from the poaching syrup and gently tease it open slightly. Now carefully spoon just enough clotted cream into the cavity to fill it, then top with a walnut half and set the filled apricot on a serving platter. Rinse your teaspoon in the hot water and repeat until all the apricots are filled. Serve immediately, or refrigerate until you are ready to serve.

Index

a

almonds
    in *baklava* 210
    in bejeweled rice 60
    cinnamon & citrus pastry cigars 220–1
    fig & green bean salad 175
    in red rice salad 181
    with rice pudding 231
    spiced carrot, pistachio & almond cake 209
apple & fennel salad 176–7
apricots 92–3, 232–3
artichoke & chicken salad 172–3
ash-e-anar 96–7
asparagus, harissa-marinated 192–3

b

baghala ghatogh 10–11
baklava 210–11
bamia 76–7
barberries
    in bejeweled rice 60
    in Persian herb frittata 27
    red rice salad with vegetables & almonds 181
    saffron-chicken & fennel stew 82–3
barley salad with za'atar & broccolini 152–3
basil 217, 222–3
bastilla, chicken 106–7
batinjan al rahib 24–5
beans, cannellini, salad 162–3
beans, green, & fig salad 174–5
beef
    kotlet, spiced 42–3
    meatballs, mini 86
    pastries, Safavid-style 38–9
    seared, with pomegranate & balsamic dressing 130–1
beet, root vegetable cakes 186–7
biryani, lamb 72–3
börek 32–3
bread
    focaccia 52–3
    Persian flatbread 54–5, 183
broccolini, in barley salad 152–3
bulgar
    salad 164–5
    tabbouleh & pomegranate 158–9

    tomato 66–7
butternut squash
    lamb, prune & tamarind tagine 94–5
    pistachio, feta & pomegranate 198–9
    spiced vegetable soup 78
    za'atar roasted, with spiced yogurt & pickled chilies 204–5

c

cacik 15
cakes 208–9, 228–9
cardamom 72, 210, 224, 231, 232
carrots
    cumin-roasted, with honey-lemon dressing & goat cheese 190–1
    lamb tagine 86
    pistachio & coconut cake 208–9
    in root vegetable cakes 186–7
chermoula, eggplant 12–13
cherries, sour, in meatballs 116–17
chicken
    & artichoke salad 172–3
    bastilla 106–7
    harissa & preserved lemon roasted poussins 110–11
    kabab, saffron & lemon *joojeh* 114–15
    olivieh salad 170–1
    ras el hanout wraps 108–9
    saffron & rosemary fillets 104–5
    stew
        saffron, fennel & barberry 82–3
        walnut & pomegranate 84–5
    tagine, preserved lemon & olive 80–1
chickpeas 28–9, 78
chili
    & herb drizzle 125
    pickled 17, 144, 184–5, 204
    pul biber 45, 122, 163
chives 27, 35, 58, 96, 173
cilantro
    baked eggs, feta & tomato 41
    in French lentil & quinoa salad 157
    herb & chili drizzle 125
    in herb frittata 27
    herb oil 78
    lamb & sour cherry meatballs 117
    & lemon hummus 28

in marinated feta 17
olive & lemon relish 144
in *olivieh* salad 170–1
Persian herb rice 58
in pesto 198
in pistachio & feta dip 36
in pomegranate soup 96
in red rice salad 181
in spiced yogurt 204
sumac, lemon & garlic shrimp 136
tamarind & fenugreek sauce 135
clams, seafood & saffron stew 98–9
coconut, spiced carrot & pistachio cake 208–9
cod
    salt cod fritters 34–5
    in tamarind, cilantro & fenugreek sauce 134–5
    za'atar, with relish 144–5
cream
    clotted, with syrup-poached apricots 232–3
    Eastern Mess 222–3
    pistachio ice cream 226–7
    rosewater 209
croutons 53, 183
cucumber
    in *fattoush* salad 183
    radish & red onion salad 154–5
    in *Shirazi* salad 178–9
    yogurt, garlic & dill 14–15
    yogurt & mint 20–1
cumin 78, 119, 125, 190–1

d

dam pokht 72
dates
    chicken *bastilla* 107
    date molasses 175
    & tamarind sauce 186
desserts 208–33
dill
    cucumber yogurt 15, 20
    with cumin-roasted carrots 191

fava beans, garlic & eggs 10
in fennel & apple salad 176
herb oil 78
lamb & sour cherry meatballs 117
Persian herb frittata 27
Persian herb rice 58
in pesto 198
in pistachio & feta dip 36
& pistachio sugar 213
salt cod fritters 35
dips 30–1, 36–7, 203
dressings
    date molasses 175
    honey & orange 181
    honey-lemon 191
    lemon & sumac 157
    mint & orange blossom 154
    pomegranate molasses 150
    saffron, honey & citrus 143
    yogurt 152, 170, 173

e

egg
    baked, with feta, harissa, tomato sauce & cilantro 40–1
    with fava beans & garlic 10–11
    in chicken *bastilla* 107
    in *olivieh* salad 170–1
    Persian herb frittata 26–7
    in smoked eggplants 18
eggplant
    chermoula 12–13
    Persian *kashk* 188–9
    Persian smoked 18–19
    in red rice salad 181
    with saffron yogurt, parsley & pickled chilies 184–5
    smoked salad 24–5
    stuffed, with lamb, garlic & tomatoes 102–3
ezme 30–1

f

fattoush salad 182–3
fava beans, garlic, dill & eggs 10–11
fennel

& apple salad 176–7
saffron-chicken & barberry stew 82–3
with scallops 142–3
feta
    with baked eggs, harissa, tomato sauce & cilantro 40–1
    with butternut squash, pistachio & pomegranate 198–9
    in chicken & artichoke salad 173
    marinated 16–17
    & pistachio dip 36–7
    sigara börek peynir 32–3
    spiced vegetable soup 78
fig & green bean salad 174–5
fistikli kebap 127
flatbread, Persian 54–5, 183
focaccia, eastern-style 52–3
frittata, Persian herb 26–7
fritters
    lacy saffron 212–13
    salt cod 34–5

g

garlic 10, 15, 102, 136, 196
    black, lamb & tomato tagine 88
    roasted, with sweet potato 203
ghelyeh mahi 135
goat cheese, with cumin-roasted carrots 190–1
grains
    barley 152
    bulgar 66–7, 158–9, 164–5
    quinoa 156–7, 168–9
    rice 58, 60, 63, 65, 68, 72

h

harissa
    with baked eggs, feta, tomato sauce & cilantro 40–1
    marinated asparagus 192–3
    & preserved lemon roasted poussins 110–11

herbs
    & chili drizzle 125
    French lentil & quinoa salad 157
    herb oil 78
    Persian frittata 26–7
    Persian herb rice 56–9
    pesto 198
hummus 28–9

i

ice cream, pistachio, honey & orange
    blossom 226–7
ingredients 6, 7

k

karniyarik 102–3
kashk, eggplants 188–9
kaymak 232
kebab
    lamb & pistachio 127
    saffron & lemon chicken *joojeh*
        114
    Turkish Adana *köfte* 122–3
kefta 46–7
Khan, Asma 72
khoresh-e-fesenjan 85
khoresh-e-gheymeh 90–1
kisir 165
köfte 122
kotlet, spiced 42–3
kuku sabzi 26–7

l

lahmacun 44–5
lamb
    bamia 76–7
    biryani 72–3
    chops, tray-baked with herb & chili
        drizzle 124–5
    kebabs, Turkish Adana *köfte* 122–3
    kefta, spiced 46–7
    lahmacun 44–5
    leg, *mechouia*-style, with cumin
        dipping salt 118–19
    meatballs 86, 116–17
    patties, with pistachio 126–7
    rack, spiced, with pomegranate sauce
        120–1

    shank, black garlic & tomato tagine
        88–9
    shoulder, spice-perfumed 128–9
    stew
        dried lime & split pea 90–1
        spiced, with apricots 92–3
    stuffed eggplants, garlic & tomatoes
        102–3
    tagine
        butternut squash, prune &
            tamarind 94–5
        with mixed vegetable 86–7
leeks, spiced vegetable soup 78
lemon
    & cilantro hummus 28
    & pistachio shortbreads 214–16
    preserved 80, 91, 110, 140, 144, 168–9
    & saffron chicken *joojeh* kabab 114–15
    in salad dressing 173, 176, 183
    sumac, cilantro & garlic shrimp 136
    & sumac dressing 157
lentils 64–5, 156–7
lettuce 158–9, 183
lime
    in *baklava* 210
    cinnamon & citrus almond pastry
        cigars 220–1
    citrus spiced salmon 138
    dried, lamb & split pea stew 90–1
    powder 128, 138

m

mahi shekampor 140
meatballs
    lamb & sour cherry 116–17
    mini 96
    Turkish *köfte* kebabs 122–3
mechouia-style lamb leg 118–19
meringues 222–3
mezze 10–49
mint
    in bulgar salad 165
    in chicken & artichoke salad
        173
    & cucumber yogurt 20
    in *fattoush* salad 183
    in French lentil & quinoa salad
        157

herb & chili drizzle 125
& orange blossom dressing
154
in pomegranate soup 96
with quinoa salad 168
in *sigara börek peynir* 33
in spiced yogurt 204
sugar 217
in yogurt sauce 109
mirza ghasemi 18–19
mojardara 64–5
monkfish, *bandari* tails 146–7
morassa polow 60
mussels, seafood & saffron stew
98–9

O

okra, *bamia* 76–7
olives 80–1, 144
olivieh salad 170–1
onions
in barley salad with za'atar &
broccolini 152
in chicken *bastilla* 107
crispy, with rice & lentils 64–5
in lamb biryani 72
Persian *kashk* eggplants
188–9
in pomegranate soup 96
red, in chicken & artichoke
salad 173
radish & cucumber salad 154–5
in tomato bulgar 66
Turkish white bean salad 163
saffron & lemon chicken *joojeh*
kabab 114
in spiced vegetable soup 78
orange
in *baklava* 210
blossom, pistachio & honey ice
cream 226–7
blossom & mint dressing 154
cinnamon & citrus almond
pastry cigars 220–1
citrus spiced salmon 138
& radicchio salad 150–1
saffron & honey vinaigrette
143

P

parsley
in bulgar salad 165
in chicken & artichoke salad
173
in *fattoush* salad 183
French lentil & quinoa salad
157
herb oil 78
in Persian herb frittata 27
in Persian herb rice 58
in pesto 198
in pomegranate soup 96
in red rice salad 181
in salt cod fritters 35
in seafood & saffron stew
98–9
in spiced lamb *kefta* 46
in spicy tomato & pepper dip
30
in *tabbouleh* 159
in Turkish white bean salad
163
pastry, filo
baklava 210
chicken *bastilla* 107
cinnamon & citrus almond
cigars 220–1
sigara börek peynir 32–3
pastry, puff, Safavid-style beef
pastries 38–9
patties
lamb & pistachio 126–7
root vegetable 186–7
spiced beef *kotlet* 42–3
see also fritters; *kofta*
pears, poached 224–5
peas, in *olivieh* salad 170–1
peppers
in *fattoush* salad 183
in red rice salad 181
in tomato bulgar 66
tomato salad 160
& tomato spicy dip 30–1
pesto, with butternut squash
198
pickles, *olivieh* salad 170–1
pine nuts 46, 107, 140, 154

pineapple & strawberry carpaccio
217–19
pistachio
in *baklava* 210
in bejeweled rice 60
with butternut squash, feta &
pomegranate 198–9
carrot & coconut cake 208–9
& dill sugar with saffron
fritters 212–13
Eastern Mess 222–3
& feta dip 36–7
herb oil 78
honey & orange blossom
ice cream 226–7
& lamb patties 126–7
& lemon shortbreads 214–16
with quinoa salad 168–9
with rice pudding 231
rose & raspberry madeleines
228–9
pita bread, croutons 183
piyaz 163
pizza, *lahmacun* 44–5
pomegranate
& balsamic dressing with beef
130–1
in bulgar salad 165
butternut squash, pistachio
& feta 198–9
chicken & walnut stew 85
with fennel & apple salad 176–7
molasses 30, 85, 96, 109, 120,
130, 133, 150, 160
& quince glazed pork 133
sauce 120
in *Shirazi* salad 178–9
soup, with mini meatballs 96–7
tabbouleh cups 158–9
tomato salad 160–1
pork, quince & pomegranate
glazed 132–3
potato
in *olivieh* salad 170–1
in root vegetable cakes 186–7
in salt cod fritters 34–5
in spiced beef *kotlet* 43
in spiced vegetable soup 78

turmeric & cumin roasted 200–1
prunes, in lamb tagine 94–5
pul biber 45, 122, 163

q

quince paste 48, 132–3
quinoa salad 156–7, 168–9

r

radicchio & orange salad 150–1
radish 154–5, 183
raisins, with lentils & rice 65
ras el hanout, chicken wraps 108–9
raspberries 222–3, 228–9
rice
    bejeweled 60–1
    in lamb biryani 72–3
    with lentils & crispy onions 64–5
    Persian basmati 62–3
    Persian herb 56–9
    in pomegranate soup 96
    pudding 230–1
    red, salad, with barberries, vegetables
      & almonds 180–1
    spicy shrimp 68–70
roast dishes
    lamb, spiced rack of 120–1
    lamb chops, tray-baked, with herb
      & chili drizzle 124–5
    lamb leg, *mechouia*-style 118–19
    lamb shoulder, spice-perfumed
      128–9
    pork, quince & pomegranate glazed
      132–3
    poussins, harissa & preserved lemon
      110–11
    turmeric & cumin potatoes 200–1
rose petals 20, 38, 128, 138, 231
rosewater
    & cardamom poached pears 224–5
    cinnamon & citrus almond pastry
      cigars 220–1
    cream 209
    Eastern Mess 222–3
    pistachio & raspberry madeleines
      228–9
    in rice pudding 231
rosemary 104

s

sabzi polow 56–9
saffron
    chicken, fennel & barberry stew 82–3
    honey & citrus vinaigrette, with
      scallops & fennel 143
    lacy fritters, with pistachio & dill sugar
      212–13
    in lamb biryani 72–3
    & lemon chicken *joojeh* kabab 114–15
    Persian dried lime lamb & split pea
      stew 90–1
    & rosemary chicken 104–5
    & seafood stew 98–9
    yogurt, with eggplants, parsley
      & pickled chilies 184–5
salads
    barley with za'atar & broccolini 152–3
    blood orange & radicchio 150–1
    bulgar *kisir* 164–5
    chicken & artichoke 172–3
    fattoush 182–3
    fennel & apple with dill &
      pomegranate 176–7
    French lentil & quinoa with lemon &
      sumac dressing 156–7
    olivieh 170–1
    quinoa, with pistachios, preserved
      lemons & zucchini 168–9
    radish, cucumber & red onion 154–5
    red rice with barberries,
      vegetables & almonds 180–1
    Shirazi 178–9
    smoked eggplant 24–5
    tabbouleh with pomegranate 158–9
    tomato 160–1
    Turkish white bean 162–3
salmon, citrus spiced 138–9
salt, cumin dipping 119
scallions
    belly-stuffed trout 140
    in *fattoush* salad 183
    in Persian frittata 27
    Persian herb rice 58
    in salads 157, 170
    salt cod fritters 35
    in spiced root vegetable cakes 186
scallops 98–9, 142–3

seafood & saffron stew 98–9
sheer berenj 231
Shirazi salad 178–9
shortbread, pistachio & lemon
214–16
shrimp
seafood & saffron stew 98–9
spicy rice 68–70
with sumac, cilantro, lemon
& garlic 136–7
sigara börek peynir 32–3
soups 78–9, 96–7
split peas 90–1, 96
squash *see* butternut squash
squid 48–9, 98–9
stews
bamia 76–7
chicken 82–3, 84–5
lamb 90–1, 92–3
seafood & saffron 98–9
see also tagine
strawberry & pineapple carpaccio
217–19
sugar, herb 213, 217
sumac
on focaccia 53
with lamb 127, 128
with shrimp 136
in salads 150, 157, 160, 173,
178, 183
with salmon 138
in tomato & pepper dip 30
in yogurt sauce 109, 204
sweet potato purée with garlic
202–3

t̛
tabbouleh with pomegranate
158–9
tagine
chicken, preserved lemon
& olive 80–1
lamb, butternut squash, prune
& tamarind 94–5
lamb & mixed vegetable 86–7
lamb shank, garlic & tomato
88–9
see also stews

tahdig 59, 60, 63, 69
tahini 28, 163
tamarind paste 94, 135, 186
tomato
bamia 76–7
in barley salad with za'atar
& broccolini 152
bulgar 66
in eggplant *chermoula* 12–13
in *fattoush* salad 183
with feta, baked eggs, harissa
& cilantro 40–1
in French lentil & quinoa salad
157
gavurdagi salatasi 160–1
lamb shank & black garlic
tagine 88–9
& pepper spicy dip 30–1
sauce, with lamb & sour cherry
meatballs 117
seafood & saffron stew 98–9
in *Shirazi* salad 178–9
spiced vegetable soup 78
in stuffed eggplants 102–3
& tray-roasted zucchinis
196–7
trout, belly-stuffed 140–1
turnips, lamb tagine 86

v
veal, mini meatballs 86

w
walnuts
in chicken & artichoke salad
173
in chicken & pomegranate
stew 85
in Persian herb frittata 27
in Persian smoked eggplants
18
with syrup-poached apricots
232
in tomato salad 160
in yogurt, cucumber & mint
20
watercress 130, 173

wraps, chicken, *ras el hanout*
108–9

y
yogurt
with cucumber, garlic & dill
14–15
cucumber & mint 20–1
dressing 152, 170, 173
in lacy saffron fritters 213
saffron, with eggplants,
parsley & pickled chilies
184–5
saffron & lemon chicken *joojeh*
kabab 114
sauce, with chicken wraps 109
spiced, with za'atar squash
204–5

z
za'atar 144–5, 152, 204
zoolbia 214
zucchini
in lamb tagine 86
with quinoa salad, pistachios
& preserved lemons 168–9
in red rice salad 181
in spiced vegetable soup 78
tray-roasted, with garlic &
tomato 196–7

Acknowledgments

I'd like to thank a handful of amazing people that I am fortunate enough to have been surrounded by... the first and foremost is my agent Martine Carter at Sauce Management, who, by some minor miracle, saw something in me enough to take me under her wing. Also to Nicky Hancock and Jo Barnes at Sauce Communications who have been incredibly supportive and kind to me, and also to Maureen Mills at Network London for being a good friend, advisor, and champion of my career.

To the lovely people at Natoora and Belazu who have supported my supper clubs and events with their wonderful products.

To Kaori Tatebayashi Ceramics for the loan of props.

To the wonderful team at Octopus Publishing, especially Stephanie Jackson and Fiona Smith who made my dream a reality, and all the passionate people they have brought in to work on this project with me. Special thanks to everyone, but especially Sybella, Jonathan, Jazzy Fizzle, and my lobster Kat Mead—who made all the brown stuff look pretty with the help of two amazing photographers, Liz and Max Haarala Hamilton, who helped me capture the true image of Middle Eastern food. Without all of you, I would not have enjoyed the process nearly as much... or the Boursin-smeared bagels and many, many meatballs. Thank you for putting your all into this book.

Last, but by no stretch of the imagination least... To my darling Emanuele... always patient, always kind... always hungry. I didn't know what was missing, until you gave it to me. Supportive, gentle, loving, and proud (even when I have been a workaholic pain in the ass)—thank you for being my tower of strength and always standing proudly by my side.

Sabrina Ghayour

First American edition published in 2015 by
INTERLINK BOOKS
an imprint of Interlink Publishing Group, Inc.
46 Crosby Street
Northampton, Massachusetts 01060
www.interlinkbooks.com

Library of Congress Cataloging-in-Publication Data
Ghayour, Sabrina.
Persiana : recipes from the Middle East & beyond / by Sabrina Ghayour.
    pages cm
Includes index.
ISBN 978-1-56656-995-8
1. Cooking, Middle Eastern. 2. Cooking, International. I. Title.
TX725.M628G43 2015
641.5956--dc23
                    2014021227

Printed and bound in China

Publisher: Stephanie Jackson
Senior editor: Sybella Stephens
American edition editor: Leyla Moushabeck
Art director: Jonathan Christie
Designer: Jaz Bahra
Photography: Liz & Max Haarala Hamilton
Illustrations: Susan Brinkhurst
Home economy: Sabrina Ghayour & Kat Mead
Food styling: Kat Mead
Assistant production manager: Lucy Carter
Proofreader: Jennifer Staltare